PUNK
LEADERSHIP

KEZIAH FEATHERSTONE

PUNK LEADERSHIP

LEading Schools Differently

CORWIN

1 Oliver's Yard
55 City Road
London EC1Y 1SP

2455 Teller Road
Thousand Oaks,
California 91320

Unit No 323-333, Third Floor, F-Block
International Trade Tower Nehru Place
New Delhi 110 019

8 Marina View Suite 43-053
Asia Square Tower 1
Singapore 018960

British Library Cataloguing in Publication data

A catalogue record for this book is available from the British Library

Editor: James Clark
Assistant Editor: Esosa Otabor
Production Editor: Gourav Kumar
Copyeditor: Rosemary Campbell
Proofreader: Sarah Cooke
Indexer: Cathryn Pritchard
Marketing Manager: Dilhara Attygalle
Cover Design: Wendy Scott
Typeset by KnowledgeWorks Global Ltd
Printed in the UK by
CPI Group (UK) Ltd, Croydon CR0 4YY

ISBN 978-1-5296-2148-8
ISBN 978-1-5296-2147-1 (pbk)

Contents

About the Author

Keziah Featherstone is a co-founder, trustee and strategic leader for #WomenEd and a member of the Headteachers' Roundtable, a non-political educational think tank. After twenty years in senior leadership, she currently she lives with her husband, daughter, three cats and three pugs in the West Midlands, where she is proud to be Executive Headteacher of Q3 Academy Tipton, a part of the Mercian Trust, her second headship. Keziah has written English educational resources for Pearson and Teachit, as well as articles for publications such as *Tes*, *The Guardian* and *Schools Week*, she also co-edited *10% Braver: Inspiring Women to Lead Education* and *Being 10% Braver*. She really likes punk.

Foreword

Captain Sensible

I can still recall the surprised faces at my primary school when the all-important 11 Plus exam results were announced – teachers expressing shock that I had somehow, despite apparently going through every lesson in a complete day-dream, gotten through. The truth was I had very little interest in the stuff being taught – today's generation would be incredulous to hear about the hours and hours 'boomers' had to endure learning nonsense related to the glories of the British Empire and reigns of various kings and queens. Boy, was being force fed that twaddle a chore, so much so that I've made a point of getting my own back by writing regular snarky songs about these strangely enduring national parasites.

But back to the surprise exam pass – achieved, I was told, due to my outlandish story in the 'composition' section. There's an annual competition at a pub in Cumbria called 'The World's Greatest Liar'. I've often thought it something that I might like to enter. Creativity can take a multitude of forms and being able to string together a few sentences, added to a naturally rebellious nature, put me in pole position when a particularly manic new music scene erupted in 1976.

Actually, I'm missing out the most important 'talent', the one that got me a place in The Damned *and* the daft stage name that has served me so well over the last few decades, which is an unfeasibly high embarrassment threshold. Basically, I don't give a hoot what anyone thinks – a fact that many attendees of The Damned's performances would attest to. In fact, some of the more scurrilous episodes would've definitely 'gone viral' if there had been a TikTok to post on back in the day.

Along with my anarchic comrade Rat Scabies I found that instigating chaos could be a lot of fun… and that I was quite good at it. Disrupting gigs became a regular thing at venues around Croydon where one would sometimes let rip with a pea shooter (I was an avid Dennis the Menace fan) when it seemed the performer was getting a bit too up themselves. During their show at the Fairfield Halls the guitarist of Manfred Mann's Earth Band got some of this treatment with his soloing dragging on to what seemed like an eternity – he got a face full of dried peas at full force and hilariously (to me anyway) threw the guitar off in disgust, stomping off the stage shaking his head at the ignominy.

A natural rebel, I hate being told what to do – what other kind of employment could I have found if punk rock hadn't arrived at exactly the right time to save me from a life of drudge and getting up every morning at 6am? Staying up all night and sleeping all day appealed more, and even better – all the beer is free when you're twangin' a guitar for a living. Of course, I was incredibly lucky, and sometimes wonder what I might have done had punk not arrived when it did because it's all very well going down the 'creative or bust' route but what happens if you don't crack it? It sure as hell don't sound like fun to be permanently stuck on the bottom rung of life's ladder, cadging off others, sleeping on people's sofas, nicking drinks in pubs, but that was basically the lifestyle I was slipping into before joining The Damned.

Then one summer, having nicked a car, I ended up in Brighton, a sleazy town I felt right at home in so stayed on for forty fairly wacky years. I managed to survive that first year with zero money pretty much – sleeping in beach huts or squats with only the clothes I was wearing to my name. Sustenance came courtesy of supermarket dustbins where all the expired products could be snaffled. So one night dinner might be stale bread, fish paste and yoghurt, the next evening, cabbage, prunes and margarine. Try knocking up edible dishes from that – and no Ainsley Harriott to help you either.

But a lot of the people you meet when living 'on the street' have amazing stories to tell, and amongst the various junkies and dropouts I met witches, con men, thieves, barristers, wannabe Hells Angels, murderers, faith healers, many of whom preferred a life of freedom away from normal society and its conformity, rules and restrictions. I found I got on with this bunch of life's outsiders better than trying to do the straight thing living at home with the parents, getting up for work like clockwork every morning only to get bossed around by some jumped up moron who enjoys dishing out orders.

So, this was the dishevelled oik that Brian James thought worth recruiting into the band he was putting together to shake up the music scene. The fact that I could play a bit helped of course, but it was the *attitude* he was primarily interested in because The Damned was essentially a gang of stroppy misfits who channelled their aggression through the music – we didn't care whether audiences loved or hated us, as long as there was a reaction.

Since those early days, The Damned has gone through a lot of changes, incorporating goth and garage psych into the sound, but along with the fans who *do* like us there's plenty of people out there who still loathe the band and that suits us fine. They can bugger off and listen to their Coldplay or Taylor Swift or whatever!

Today's UK is a very different country than the one I was growing up in in the 1960s. Of course, as a confirmed old fart I'm not going to pretend I understand what's going on but there's a new generation who have to make head or tail of it all now – but I sometimes wonder what on Earth I'd do with myself if just leaving school now. What *are* the current options for youngsters in a job market dominated by government austerity programmes and the unrelenting march of anti-worker technology?

History is strewn with arty types who kept their heads above water financially care of some humdrum day job or other while pursuing their creative muse ... my namesake, the mega poet Robert Burns (think Auld Lang Syne, etc.) was a lowly customs officer – the traffic warden of his day. Bo Diddley a carpenter. Vivaldi a priest. Agatha Christie a pharmacist. Mick Jagger a hospital porter. You gotta pay the bills, ain't ya and yours truly saved up for his music equipment by working for a while as a bog cleaner – possibly the shittest of shit jobs!

So, what do you do in this day and age of AI making many decently paid occupations redundant? Maybe play it crafty? Look at the occupations that Silicon Valley's clever algorithms, robots and automation will *never* be able to replace and learn enough of those skills that you can still have your fun painting, writing poetry or making a horrible racket with a guitar while still having some sort of lifestyle. Hedge your bets if you like, so, tedious as it sounds, we are talking about plumber, electrician, carpenter, dentist, farmer, sportsman, roofer, cleaner.

Stick that in your pipe Bill Gates!

Smash It Up

Acknowledgements

I'd like to acknowledge every person who is going to hate the concept and principles of this book; I probably stand by every word I've written here but I'm very likely to have forgotten what I've said. To be clear, if you hate my choice of tracks, these are not my favourite punk songs of all time (and I know I've really stretched the punkness a few times) but that's OK. That's punk.

I'd really like this opportunity to acknowledge the places and people that have shaped my love of punk over the decades. From the dangerous mean streets of Bradford-upon-Avon, Marshfield and Bath, to Munich, Manchester, and especially Birmingham. But not Bristol. Bristol can mostly fuck off.

Thank you: Iesha Small for unprovoked love and flattery; Hywel Roberts for being bothered; the legend that is Captain Sensible for incredible generosity. Thank you: Esosa and James for encouragement and discipline.

Thank you: Café Soya, Poly Styrene, Gianfranco Zola, Elis + John, Toni Morrison, Wilfred Owen, Malala Yousifazi, Billy Duffy, Eniola Aluko and, of course, Tait Coles.

Thank you: Emma, Mike, Claire, Ruth, Jules, Sarah, Ros, Alice, Jules, Jon, Vivienne, Sabrina, Vic and Dave for love and friendship and to every amazing dedicated colleague I've served beside and child I've encountered.

Thank you: mum and dad for enduring all those mix-tapes ('The Cure would be OK if he didn't start singing'); and Andy and Evie as, it makes me glad to say / It's been a lovely day and it's okay.

Thank you: to every kid.

Anger is an energy: use it.

Reader's Note

This book contains swearing and punk rock. If either offends this may not be the book for you. For everyone else, hey ho, let's go!

Reader's Note

Introduction – Lust For Life

Iesha Small

Keziah is a wonderful empathetic person hiding behind a grumpy cow persona. She starts *Punk Leadership* saying she hates people – when I know for a fact that she cares deeply about many people, her students, her staff, her friends and family. She also cares about the English education system and her fellow school leaders, which is why she wrote the book, for people just like you. Keziah does hate dicks to be fair, but I think that's fine.

I've known Keziah for many years, back when she started WomenEd. I've worked with leaders at her school, stayed at her house and been woken up by her unreasonably loud hamsters. Keziah is punk. She's anti-establishment and irreverent which I find hilarious for somebody who is a headteacher and tells other people what to do.

At one point in my career I was an assistant headteacher. I looked around at the heads I knew and it didn't look much fun for most of them so I decided that route wasn't the best for me. Keziah might be one of the few heads I know who makes the job look fun. Even though she initially presents as grumpy to strangers, her zest and lust for life and education shine through.

Maybe if I'd read this book, and more people around me had taken Keziah's advice about happy talk, I may have seen a path for myself and stayed on in school senior leadership. I'm so glad that Keziah has written this book. As a school leader you have the chance to make a real difference. The feeling of accountability can sometimes get you down but, she's right, you don't have to be anybody's dog. Your school is its own ecosystem, its own world. You can create a happy house where your staff and pupils thrive.

Any leadership book that has 'Here's a bitch who'll give it back' as a heading (Chapter 5) is not for cookie-cutter people. If you are a values-driven leader who likes to do things differently Keziah has written this for you.

You don't need to be a punk fan to love this book. I grew up listening to hip hop and reggae myself but there is plenty of crossover. All are types of protest music. All are made by people who felt excluded by mainstream society and told the truth in a way that made sense to them. That's the ethos of this book. Truth telling. Using what you have to make a difference. Getting things done. Saying never mind the bollocks, let's do what really matters.

I interviewed Keziah for my own book, *The Unexpected Leader*, a few years ago. She generously spoke of her own experiences of depression at a time before it was acceptable to do so in education leadership books. It was so unusual that I kept her anonymous. In *Punk Leadership*, Keziah has written more about mental health. She outlines the stresses of being a school leader and how, if you are not careful, it can make you live dead. She gives key suggestions on that topic and others throughout the book to keep you on course.

If you care about your students and staff ...

If you worry about the 'us and them' in education ...

Don't worry you aren't alone. Use *Punk Leadership* to help you lead with a lust for life.

Display this book proudly. Other current and aspiring punk leaders will see it and know what you stand for.

Read this rousing book.

Feel energised to lead.

Disrupt the establishment.

Safety pins and spiky hair are optional.

1
I Hate People

Punk Leadership Principles

This is not a book about school improvement.

There's bloody loads of them.

Someone once told me that the concept of me writing a book about school improvement was 'ludicrous and laughable'. I don't hate *all* people but I certainly hated him because, as someone who was a school leader, he should have known better.

This *is* a book about leading in schools and striving to be a better leader. It is a book about deliberately making decisions to be part of the anti-nowhere league; to actively choose a space within leadership where your principles are firm and precise. To choose not to be wedged between two somethings – not sitting on the fence if you will. Nowhere is a terrible place to be in education because others will certainly try to put you somewhere that you wouldn't choose to be, be it colleagues, children, parents or agencies such as Ofsted or the government. You need to hold on to your values if you're not going to go bonkers.

That is not to say you cannot change your mind if the evidence or experience suggests that you should; nothing lasts forever. However, flip-flopping between nothingness helps no one, even more so if you do so merely to appease others or follow fads and fashions. Following a rubric established by others can sometimes work but school leadership rarely comes flat-packed and easily assembled. It's messy and you're going to make mistakes.

Joe Strummer, of The Clash said, 'Punk rock isn't something you grow out of. Punk rock is an attitude, and the essence of that attitude is "give us some truth"'.

And that is the same for punk leadership. It is not about anarchy or chaos. It is not about pink hair and piercings and Dr Martens (although they can play a part, see Chapter 22).

It is about being driven by your values to make a difference and to get stuff done. Sitting in an office talking about strategy only gets you so far – you have to get out there and do it, even if it's hard, because it is *always* important. You are working everyday with the most important people on the planet, the next generation, and, as well as only having one chance at school, for many it is difficult, confusing, frustrating and alien to them. You can talk all you like about cultural capital, social mobility and levelling up but it is empty rhetoric unless you actually *do* something about it.

Punk leadership is also not about being an 'authentic leader' because that is absolutely no use to anyone if your authentic self is being a bit of a dick. If being a dick is your authentic self then I would urge you *not* to be an authentic leader but to fake being a professional, empathetic leader instead.

When I first started teaching I only wanted to teach and I wanted to be the best teacher I could be. Pretty soon though I got annoyed by some of what I was being asked to do, especially when no one could explain why I needed to do it. So, I looked to those immediately above me in the leadership chain and thought, I can do that and maybe I should – if I do this job, I can tell myself what to do instead of that person. It was my battle against the nowhere league. And essentially that's how I ended up in each successive role and am now an executive headteacher.

Most importantly, punk leadership is about people, not policies; it is about children and doing everything to ensure their entire lives get better through providing a safe, secure environment so that they learn and become confident successful adults … and that's also pretty difficult to do as parents. It is also about the adults that you work alongside, because feeling valued and appreciated, developed and supported in your work is essential for anyone, regardless of their role. By extension, punk leadership also has a commitment to all the adults in our students' lives, even if they're on Facebook slagging us off. It's a responsibility to create a school free from bullshit and very definitely anti-nowhere by design.

Hide Away

There have been many times as a school leader where, as Anti-Nowhere League sang in 1982, it's all about finding a quiet room and bashing your brains on the wall. Schools, and the wider education sector, are full of people that will drive you crazy – and I don't mean the children.

Truthfully, I don't really like people. These days I'd be classed as an introvert; most think of me as a miserable cow and that's OK. 'Are you alright Miss?' someone will ask and I will reply 'everything aches; just wait until you're a menopausal middle-aged woman too'. Usually the Year 7 boy simply looks confused.

Introverts leading schools have to pretend to be outgoing, confident and cheerful on a regular basis and that is exhausting. The whole interviewing process, and presenting yourself as positive and outgoing can feel like torture; maintaining this for the whole job is excruciating: assemblies, presentations, meetings, Ofsted, parents' evenings … But there is no alternative because the job and the school are unbelievably important. Some people do feel tortured, but you can't always just shut the door to your office and grunt when it's knocked on.

This is not dissimilar to being a teacher. When I made the decision that I wanted to teach, it was as if I forgot, or blanked out, the whole requirement to stand up in front of up to 35 teenagers, manage their behaviour and ensure they learnt things without any Jedi mind tricks. I didn't really want to speak, or raise my voice, or even insist on the students doing anything initially. Unsurprisingly it didn't go well. I resorted to scripting lessons so I had something to work from but there is nothing like a classroom to go off script. With practice, encouragement and after making a lot of mistakes I got better. Now, I can walk into a classroom without hours of preparation, so long as I am familiar with the content, and do well. Now, I prefer to riff it, to improvise, as I am now confident enough to know my overly scripted lessons severely limited what the class and I could achieve together. Now, I am more confident to respond to the needs of my students as they arise.

And this is the same with being an introverted leader. Over time I did not metamorphosise from an introverted to an extroverted teacher – experience and practice enabled me to develop the skills required to fake it; the journey was exactly the same for being a leader.

Bang my Brains

As a secondary English teacher my first steps into positional leadership were within the curriculum area. Teachers, especially English teachers, are not easy to lead and manage and I found this out the hard way. I was also not very good at managing the far more experienced middle-aged women that comprised the department, was probably a little irritating and cocky to people who really did not want to change what they'd been doing for the last 20 years and I certainly took things far too seriously. I let myself get upset and often spent nights awake worrying about things said. With hindsight they were far more gentle than other colleagues I have worked with.

I certainly understood the need to identify what needed to change and *why* rather than just because I fancied it. I understood that anything new being introduced worked best if my colleagues could see what was in it for them, or even better if they felt changing something was their idea. This is not to suggest that I thought that tricking people was the best policy, rather if we could all independently come to the same outcome that really helped what we were trying to achieve. Ultimately, if anything needed changing it needed changing for the students.

When I got my first promotion to senior leadership, which was in the school I'd been head of department in for several years, things really changed. Colleagues who had once been very friendly with me, going out for beers together and having a sing or cry together at the end of term, now referred to me as part of the *they*. *They* want us to do this … *They* told me to … *They* want everyone to… *They* think … Suddenly I was the other, the enemy, and the senior leader position isolated me from those that now thought I wanted to be their superior whilst also solving all their problems. Some really personal and aggressive written feedback after a training session I led from someone who I'd previously considered a friend, absolutely floored me. It was as if the perception was that now I was a senior leader I was a nefarious robotic dictator with no feelings. That day I certainly wanted to 'hide away / And find a wall to bang my brains'. My then headteacher told me to keep the feedback safe and take it out and look at it on occasion and one day I would feel differently about it. I never did, I still don't 15 years later.

In a profession where there is so much to unite us, and given that the days and terms can be unbelievably hard, it genuinely grieves me that there is so often conflict between educators. These days, as a far more experienced leader, I now expect a certain amount of hate from all directions: within school, in the community, from the press, from government and on social media. It saddens me but I tend not to worry about it as much. Helping new senior leaders navigate this challenge is something I spend a lot of time doing as, like becoming a new parent, you can brace yourself knowing what's coming but it's different when it's happening to you.

That's not to say that I am unaware of school leaders who are less than pleasant and do not treat others with dignity, humanity or kindness. Indeed, it was this overtly macho bullish model of being a leader that brought a group of women together to set up WomenEd and challenge this concept, promoting an alternative leadership approach for everyone.

Joey Ramone said, 'Punk is about being an individual and going against the grain and standing up and saying "this is who I am."' Being a punk leader means turning your back on unethical and inhumane ways of treating others, of refusing to let children become wholly examination statistics, and standing up to those that would do so. Leadership should always be kind, even if those you're being kind to are determined to make you the villain.

This book is about what being a punk leader means to me and how as a leader I am always growing and improving as well as making mistakes. Children need brilliant adults working together in schools to support them, and they deserve the very best leaders championing them. But we have a massive recruitment and retention crisis across the whole of education, especially at leadership and headteacher level. You have only to look at the data and research to know that unbelievable pressures and toxic accountability are making the job untenable. This may lead to good, strong, ethical and humane people leaving leadership positions or never applying for them in the first place. That might be *you*. If it is you then I hope you will find enough in this book to know that you can be the kind of leader you want to be and we need you!

Remember the passion and vision that inspired you to work in education in the first place and hold on to that tightly: that's your punk and, to repeat Joe Strummer's words from the start of this chapter,

> Punk rock isn't something you grow out of. Punk rock is an attitude, and the essence of that attitude is 'give us some truth'.

This book is my truth for you.

2
Career Opportunities

Establishing and Progressing your
Career as a Punk Leader

The Reluctant Career

When I was a teenager in the eighties I was fairly certain the world would end in a nuclear Armageddon; the musical landscape was filled with songs like Frankie Goes to Hollywood's 'Two Tribes', Nena's '99 Luftballons', Depeche Mode's 'Two Minute Warning', Ultravox's 'Dancing with Tears in my Eyes', Sting's 'Russians' and even Prince's 'Ronnie, Talk to Russia'. Every night our family ate dinner whilst watching the BBC's *Six O'Clock News* and that did little to alleviate my fears. I was absolutely certain we were all going to die, as I explained to my dad on a regular basis whenever he raised what I wanted to do in the future. As far as I was concerned there was no future. I certainly wasn't going to do my homework and probably got up to a fair bit of mischief I shouldn't have. My parents continued to engage with me as if the world would go on as normal.

I was lucky that I grew up in a home where people read and valued education. Neither mum nor dad went to university but they always assumed I would, to the point where I ended up thinking, *OK fuck it, go on then*. A few years later as I was finishing my degree, and definitely without thinking things through too carefully I made the decision to train as a teacher: *OK fuck it, go on then*.

Sure, there have been days when I wished I'd chosen to go into waste management, become a nail technician or learnt to play the guitar and become a famous rock star, but overwhelmingly I think I made the right decision. I love teaching; no two days are the same, kids are brilliant if infuriating and as an English teacher I get to explore my favourite texts, swapping them around when I got bored. When as Head of English I introduced A Level Film Studies I was in heaven. Yes, of course I'd love to spend a month teaching the 1920 film *Das Cabinet des Dr. Caligari*.

The difference you can make to people's lives is incredible: one previous student, by then in the army, tracked me down to write and thank me for standing up for him when he was about to be permanently excluded and since that point he'd turned his life around. I taught England striker Eniola Aluko, who was so inspired by the GCSE text *To Kill a Mockingbird* she trained as a lawyer alongside her football career. I know a former student who now teaches English and Film in the classroom I taught him those subjects in. As a teacher it is important you keep every note, card, email, message and memory safe; you need a treasure trove of happiness for the days it doesn't go so well.

Being a teacher is a career in itself and you do not have to seek promotions to be brilliant and successful. You do not have to knock on anyone's door if you don't want to. Teachers genuinely are the leaders of their own classrooms and if you don't want added responsibility at all, or right now, you're not letting anyone down.

At the same time there is an abundance of roles in education if you are not a teacher, but which have just as much impact on children's lives and where you are also an essential leader: learning support assistants, pastoral teams, administration, technicians, school business and finance managers, human resources, site management, cleaning, health and safety … we are an interlocking net to catch and support all young people, and without one of us that net breaks.

They Offered Me the Office

But do you want to be a leader? Each step up there is not an awful lot more money, very little extra time and a great deal more responsibility and account-ability. Each step enables you to improve your leadership skills, and put them into practice rather than just studying them. Most importantly, each step allows you to have a greater impact on the experience children have at school.

For me, I kept looking upwards at those making decisions above me, arro-gantly assuming I could do better and eventually I took the plunge. You have no way of knowing if you will be any good at something until you're doing it and you also have to accept that you won't be good at it straight away. One of the most common conversations I have with people is about them knowing whether they are ready for the next step. You are never ready for it. You will always feel woefully out of your depth and when you finally feel like you know what you're doing the next opportunity calls. *OK fuck it, go on then.*

To be a leader you simply need to want to make a very real difference to all those that work in schools, not just a subsection of the community and certainly not just for the money or office. Don't worry if you're wracked with doubts, so long as you commit to constantly learning and improving you will be amazing and the kids need you.

There are so many ways to become a better leader. A growing number of courses exist such as NPQs, accreditation through the Chartered College of Teaching, the National College, Masters, doctorates, National Award of Special

Educational Needs and plenty of internal opportunities within schools, trusts and local authorities (and that's just the currently active routes in England). I think a little theory is important but you also have to learn on the job, by doing, by observing those around you and learning from what works and what doesn't. As much as I always looked above me and thought *I can do that* there have been plenty more times that I've been inspired and astounded by those I have met or worked with and thought *I can't do that!* Some have been teachers but not all, many have worked in different professions. I think the best leaders learn from everyone they come into contact with.

Who Do you Want to be?

Frequently we observe other leaders and assume that to be a leader ourselves we have to be just like them. That is untrue. Too often the stereotypical leader is pale, male and stale, which has done little for diversification in leadership teams. Children should be able to look at the adults in their schools and see themselves reflected in their faces or indeed represented in the world around them.

Do not look at other leaders you know and admire and think you are not good enough to be like them. Conversely, do not think that to be a leader you have to sell out your values and adopt appalling and unethical practices to fit in. Be punk: be yourself, do not be that other asshole. You can be the leader you want to be, one true to yourself. You can be the leader you deserved when working for someone awful, the one others now deserve. There are not enough leaders to go around – by stepping up you can be part of a movement of strong ethical leadership rather than handing it to whoever else shows up.

Ambition is good. Greed is not. The ambition to want to be better, to improve, to serve, to make a difference for more and more people is admirable. Wanting the position and title alone or to boss around others for your own ego is the very opposite of punk. An enhanced salary helps but you can't do it just for the cash. The whole profession is not based on anyone getting rich and those that do often end up in prison.

The Divide

Teachers tend to split into the two leadership camps of curriculum and pastoral in schools. Often the first promotional step is something such as a head of department or a head of year, as if this sets us on a one-directional track you can never get off. However, choosing to support young people's emotional and personal development is not completely divorced from improving their curriculum, education and outcomes. For children it's all one big school experience and they tend not to divide it, even though they know different people help them with different things. Although your role may end up being more pastoral or more curriculum it is essential that you upskill yourself to know and understand the whole school experience. Shadow others where possible, read up on it, help out as much as possible. You might be a guitarist but sometimes you might need to have a go on drums; it's all a career opportunity.

Likewise, the divide between traditional and progressive ideologies is a nonsensical division. Leaders may veer more towards one rather than the other, but within schools, which are by nature punkishly messy, adherence to a pure educational paradigm rarely works. Rather, school leadership and management is more like a world buffet where you may have preferred favourites but it's always worth trying something new to see if you like it. This is to be encouraged; how do you know whether it will work or not unless you sample it? The best music has come about by a magical amalgamation of contradictory elements that on paper shouldn't work but do.

Headship

Leading principal and media guru Vic Goddard's book about running his school is called *The Best Job in the World* – and it is. Very few serving or retired heads would claim to have aspired to the role when first starting out and that is definitely the case for me. Headship can seem so remote, so lofty, difficult and stressful that you steer clear for much of your career, never really entertaining it as a possibility until it's too late and you're hooked. Yes, I am a headteacher by mistake. Ultimately you make the decision that you want to be the architect of the best school you can imagine.

The responsibility and pressure is immense but the rewards are magnificent. The hypothetical *if I was in charge I would …* is now a reality and so long as you don't break the law you have the power to make it happen.

It is not necessarily more work; indeed, being a head may mean a reduction in actual workload as you should be delegating to others to help prepare them for their own headships. It's also where you realise there never was a pastoral/curriculum divide as you need enough knowledge of everything to effectively hold others to account regardless of their role. It also helps if you have a strong understanding of special educational needs and safeguarding. There are few schools now where you have to actively manage the money or the site, as there are business managers and Trust central services that will enable you to focus on improving outcomes, but you do need to be briefed well enough not to bankrupt your school by May.

Like every other tier of leadership, the stereotype for headship has previously been officious and remote men – this has to change to include representation from diverse backgrounds and identities. We talk about women hitting the glass ceiling, for women of colour this ceiling can be concrete or, even worse, it can be a glass cliff others will push you off. Sometimes you have to trail blaze though and change the sector from within. I don't mean to be simplistic or glib, it's bloody hard work, with personal sacrifices made. But nothing changes unless you fight for it and our next generation deserves better.

New Opportunities

Educational leadership is no longer limited to roles within schools and there are growing opportunities outside the school gates. There was always the opportunity to work for exam boards and local authorities but some really innovative opportunities are being created by multi-academy trusts both for qualified teachers and associate staff. Additionally, there are roles in government such as HMIs and working for the Department for Education. You can move tiers and I know many colleagues that were primary trained who are now working in secondary and vice versa; I have seen some move into higher education and thrive as well as some moving into private business or journalism as education experts. If it improves the lives of children it all counts.

Increasingly, working abroad looks like a very tempting option. One of my closest friends has spent her entire career moving around the world taking her family with her. After five years in Oman she went to Malaysia, saying simply, 'We did the desert so I thought let's see what the jungle is like.' If this appeals to you be very careful with the school you apply to, some locations have many pop-up, barely legal institutions and you can be badly stung. Once, a school in Singapore notified her with a week to go that their student admissions were not as anticipated and there was now no job.

A Note on Applications

When applying for a leadership role ensure you get all your dates and details completely accurate, and always name your current headteacher as a referee even if you don't like them. Yes, spelling, punctuation and grammar really matter.

Your covering statement really matters too and this should be kept to two sides, not in a font requiring a microscope to read. Avoid clichés. Present yourself as you really are. You do not want to pretend in the application form or in person that you are in any way different to who you really are. It is hell on earth having to maintain an illusion in role and if you can't be yourself you will be utterly miserable. When you present as wholly yourself, and they want you for who you are, the professional relationship will be respectful, kind and honest. If your feedback after being unsuccessful is *we don't think you are a good fit* then it's a narrow escape for everyone. Be glad they don't want you; you won't want them.

Statements should use personal pronouns (I, we) and use strong modal verbs (will, shall). Avoid listing everything in your career in chronological order and instead open with what you will do in that school to improve it; the following paragraphs should explore how your previous experiences will enable you to be successful in your new role, and be precise: by doing X it led to Y and can be further developed by Z. Emphasise impact. Punk leaders get straight to the point.

Punk leadership suggests

- There is never a good time to become a leader and you're never really ready, so do it anyway.
- Punk leaders are always themselves not someone else.
- Don't lead like a dick.
- There is no pastoral/curriculum divide, so embrace it all.
- Headship is bloody brilliant so don't dismiss it.
- There are so many new opportunities across the sector as well.
- Don't feel guilty for being ambitious and building your career.

3
I Wanna Be Your Dog
Leadership Structures and Accountability

The Godfather

I bloody love Iggy Pop. The Stooges may not have been the very first punk band but they're definitely one of the earliest. Absolutely relentless, Iggy has chameleoned his way through an exceedingly influential musical career. The son of an English teacher in Michigan, he was raised in a trailer park.

In 2007, he said:

> Once I hit junior high … I began going to school with the son of the president of Ford Motor Company, with kids of wealth and distinction. But I had a wealth that beat them all. I had the tremendous investment my parents made in me. I got a lot of care. They helped me explore anything I was interested in. This culminated in their evacuation from the master bedroom in the trailer, because that was the only room big enough for my drum kit. They gave me their bedroom.[1]

Certainly, his parents' belief, strong values and sacrifices gave the world the 'godfather of punk', who still frequently performs bare-chested even now well into his seventies. In 1987 I saw him in a double bill with The Cult in Munich. Had I not been 16 I would have realised that these things don't happen all the time and I might have drunk less Helles.

Being Accountable

Leaders serve their communities and yet are the bosses, an interesting dichotomy. We hold others to account and yet we are accountable to everyone. It's definitely a role you have to choose: you have to wanna be their dog. Being accountable is essential; how and what you improve matters and you can't just take the cash and do nothing. And you certainly can't make things worse. When we talk of toxic accountability it's not the accountability part of that we have a problem with, it's the high-stakes, knife-edge, unrealistic and relentless toxicity of some of these systems.

But who are we accountable to? As leaders we are accountable to the children in our care for their whole lives. The responsibility we have to secure their one chance at a dazzling education is not to be dismissed lightly. Of course, this does not mean that teachers or leaders should shoulder that responsibility alone, after all it takes a whole village to raise the child. It also does not mean that our students have to like us, although they certainly need to feel respected and safe with us. We won't all get an Ian Wright with Mr Pigden moment,[2] but without a doubt our most important role is to provide the very best education we can that will enable them to lead fulfilling lives.

We are also accountable to children's parents and carers, those adults who entrust their young people to us. Relationships between school and home can sometimes be fraught and challenging and occasionally hostile but at the very core we have to be committed to the same ends: the best outcomes for the young people we care about, even if we have different opinions on what those outcomes should be or how to achieve them. My experience tells me never to get into a battle of wills with parents or carers and, instead of locking horns, traverse sideways, find some common ground and identify at least one person in the school who they can talk to. Often hostility comes from fear and mistrust but positive relationships can be established over time. I can only remember one or two sets of parents that maintained aggressive distrust of a school and once all attempts to find common ground were exhausted, they ended up moving their children to different schools. This is not a failure; children deserve to attend a school where their parents are not locked in a constant battle with the other significant adults in their life. At the same time, don't take a transfer request form to the first grumpy meeting you have. Some leaders are too easily tempted to shift perceived problems to another school.

Leaders are also accountable to those above them in the structure, whatever that might mean in your own institution. The landscape in England has certainly been revolutionised since I started teaching. Regardless of your political beliefs, academies and multi-academy trusts are here to stay; the important thing is that they do not become soulless or cultish empires. We are not helpless victims entangled in these structures; choose your home carefully, do your research and leave when it's no longer something you want to be a part of. Your bosses – headteachers, chief executive officers, governors, trustees – they are also accountable to you.

Volunteering to experience those structures from a different perspective is an invaluable professional activity as well as being a decent thing to do. Consider becoming a school governor or even a trustee and work from within to make institutions fair and scrupulous; you achieve more inside the tent unless that tent should really be on fire.

Not Being Your Dog

Being accountable to someone is not the same as actually being their dog. It'll be a rare public servant that has not been told 'I pay your wages' by someone thinking that because they pay taxes they are also somehow our boss and therefore can tell us what to do. Opinions are to be welcomed but we remain the professionals, the ones who make the right decisions for the community.

We're also not accountable to the local press. Those stories that appear periodically about uniform infringements or term-time holiday fines are not about holding anyone to account; they are clickbait to generate more advertising revenue. After all, how shocking is a school with rules actually applying those rules? Rather, there is something magnetic for readers of these online articles that entertains rather than informs. They serve to reinforce already entrenched opinions about the unreasonableness of an education system the readers already don't like *or* to judge the students and parents being featured. I've heard such articles referred to as *poverty porn* as the families featured are rarely the affluent middle classes. The awful comments beneath these articles often abuse and deride the children and adults featured, which is the direct opposite of what they intended when they phoned the local paper with their story of woe.

It is for this reason that I never respond to the threat of, 'I'm going to phone the local paper' made by angry parents; other solutions to their concerns are preferable. It's their prerogative to do this of course, although I do hope that the bear-baiting appetite for such stories is waning amongst both editors and general population. Sometimes it is uncomfortable for the school but I can guarantee it pretty always backfires on the family themselves; which the paper knows when they pursue the story.

In a similar vein, the publication of results league tables of schools is abhorrent. These are shared with no context whatsoever and with an illusion of transparency and accountability. Children, and their performance in examinations, is not sport. Unless your child was at the top of any list, you would not want their individual results displayed; imagine what that would do to their self-esteem, sense of worth and ambitions for the future. Now apply that to a whole community.

My Favourite Place

External, independent accountability is vital for a healthy and trustworthy system. Whatever body it is that ultimately holds schools accountable, it should be independent and scrupulously fair. Should it be a government body? Well, I guess that depends on your view of the Department for Education and whether they are doing good work. What certainly doesn't help is ultimately being graded, having the complex and important work of schools reduced to just one of four judgements that becomes short-hand for everything your school does; at the time of writing, in England, this is the case. What parent really wants to send their child to a school that requires improvement or is inadequate? Which member of staff willingly moves to a school that has so many areas for improvement? Well, punk leaders sometimes do.

I've worked at outstanding schools that were far from perfect; places where everything humane was sacrificed for exam percentages and many vulnerable children struggled and then disappeared before census; places where staff were worked to the bone, compulsory line management at 7:00am but told *this* is what it took to maintain outstanding. And I have also worked at inadequate schools in special measures where real magic happened, not without their problems but with truly great practice and dedicated professionals working hard for amazing kids.

I moved to my current headship in 2018 after a period of disillusionment, pondering whether I should just quit the whole thing and do something else. But then this new opportunity arose – a SNOW school – a *school no one w*anted. It had been in special measures for around ten years, originally as a local authority school after which it was re-brokered to a multi-academy trust that did not seem to have its best interests at heart. After a further judgement of special measures, the school was again re-brokered, this time to a multi-academy trust I had worked with before and with a CEO I trusted. I believe the then regional schools commissioner had been looking for a new Trust for the school for a long time but no one was interested, in the context of the history of being inadequate; too many headteachers in a short period of time; high numbers of children on free school meals; a huge debt (over £1 million); and a building subject to the public finance initiative. Given the adage that headteachers can be replaced faster than football managers, who in their right mind would want to lay their career down in such a place?

At our first exploratory meeting the CEO said to me, 'There is an awful lot to do, but I'll be with you every step of the way', and she was. I know other heads who have been told at similar meetings, 'You have three years then you're out.' A visit to this school clarified to me its potential and that every single person at the school deserved better than they had previously had. One student stopped me in the corridor and said, 'Are you the person who wants to be our new headteacher? Why would you want to come somewhere like *this*?' And he seemed genuinely bewildered but also broken and resigned to always getting second or third best. I do not believe I am the best by any stretch of the imagination but I do think that punk leaders step up to serve when others shy away. I knew it would be bloody hard, completely exhausting (and this was without a global pandemic) but would be worth it. If you enter the profession to change lives and make a difference, where better than a community that everyone has given up on?

So Messed Up

Nothing we do as punk leaders should be done because of Ofsted or any other external body; what you do has to be the best decision for your school and community. Leadership is not about chasing after someone else's rainbows, as if because the school down the road was graded outstanding and they have a duck pond, by getting a duck pond you too will be outstanding. It's not the carrot with which to inspire your community and too much of 'what Ofsted wants' is open to interpretation. So just concentrate on what is right for your school and act like they don't exist.

When Ofsted recently visited us they were able to recognise the incredible progress and journey the school had made, and made a very accurate assessment of the areas we are excelling in as well as areas we need to improve further. The narrative of that inspection is fair but I also appreciate that many will reduce us to the one overall judgement without bothering with the full narrative. Sadly, I am also aware of many schools up and down the country whose experience was not as humane as ours (note: humane does not mean it wasn't intense and rigorous). External accountability that cannot be completely consistent in its judgements needs to be paused whilst it is properly reviewed; four bland statements should be removed and replaced only with a rigorous narrative report.

One perverse result of previous Ofsted practice was that schools judged as outstanding were exempt from inspection and for some this has lasted well over ten years. Ofsted's own data shows that in 2021–22 only 17% of outstanding schools re-inspected that year maintained this grade and 21% were judged as requires improvement or inadequate, although much of this has been attributed to a change in framework.[3] So long as your results looked great no one external was keeping an eye on what you did really, which is far from ideal. This is why I advocate strongly for safeguarding to be decoupled from the current inspection framework. Keeping children safe is far too important to be looked at externally just once every few years. Instead, there should be a yearly safeguarding audit, much like there is for a school's financial conduct. We pay an external independent auditor to examine our finances yearly, so why not do the same for safeguarding? Surely, children are far more important than cash?

I Wanna be Your Dog

Being a leader will always mean being a servant to others and you will always be held accountable. If you do not like or respect those holding you accountable then remember you have the agency to change that: find a new school, or trust, or sector or a completely new profession. Yes, it is that simple; we are in a recruitment and retention crisis after all.

And if the system is not operating as you believe it should then start to contribute to the changing of that system: become active in your union or professional association, become involved in grassroots movements like WomenEd, LGBTEd, BAMEed or DisabilityEd. Can't find a group that represents what you think needs to happen? Start your own. If it is important it is worth fighting for.

Punk leadership suggests

- Embracing accountability – unsupervised power is a bad thing.
- Ensure you are being held accountable by people that you trust, like and respect.
- External accountability is essential for a healthy education system but Ofsted needs serious reform.
- Never ever do anything for Ofsted; do it because it is right for the community.
- Get involved – help shape the system and how it holds us accountable.

Notes

1   Fricke, D. (2007) *Iggy Pop: The Rolling Stone Interview*. [online] Rolling Stone. Available at: https://www.rollingstone.com/music/music-news/iggy-pop-the-rolling-stone-interview-2-78680/ [Accessed 29 Jan. 2024].

2   BBC (2021) *Ian Wright's Teacher Gave Him Direction and Purpose during his Turbulent Upbringing – BBC*. YouTube. Available at: https://www.youtube.com/watch?v=6caCqn_nD6o [Accessed 29 Jan. 2024].

3   The Guardian. (2022) *Hundreds of Schools in England Lose Outstanding Status after Reinspection*. [online] Available at: https://www.theguardian.com/education/2022/nov/22/hundreds-of-schools-in-england-lose-outstanding-status-after-reinspection [Accessed 29 Jan. 2024].

4
Happy House
Building Happy Schools

Shock

When I first discovered punk I wanted to be Siouxsie; given that as a child a few years earlier I had wanted to be Elizabeth Taylor's Cleopatra this was not a huge aesthetic movement. I wanted to be a Goth Queen but my great grandma would laugh at me, 'Who do you think you are, the Queen of Sheba?' It did not help that my attempts to apply extravagant liquid eyeliner made me resemble Picasso's Dora Maar more than Siouxsie.

As well as a twenty-year career with The Banshees, subsequent bands and solo ventures, Siouxsie was celebrated for her outstanding contribution to music at the 2011 Q Awards and received the Ivor Novello inspiration award in 2012. After an unconventional childhood she developed a strong distrust of the middle-class suburbs. Siouxsie wanted to shock which led to her becoming an early devotee of The Sex Pistols. Following them to France on tour she was beaten up for wearing a Swastika armband, a move she later claimed was naively designed to simply shock and not to make any political statement. Regardless, it was bloody stupid and remains an unforgiveable transgression but one she has apologised for. Shortly after this Siouxsie and the Banshees wrote 'Mittageisen' in memory of John Heartfield, the anti-Nazi artist.

Siouxsie was on screen when Bill Grundy interviewed The Sex Pistols; when she told Grundy she had always wanted to meet him he suggested they meet after the show, this led to Steve Jones' now famous expletive driven outburst on prime-time telly.

Siouxsie remains problematic but so is the song 'Happy House'. Yes, it's about a happy house where there is 'fun fun fun' but the happiness is an illusion as they have their 'blinkers on'. When I think about happy schools there is a difference between a genuinely content community (which is never happy all the time) and somewhere with a shiny superficial gloss. I once visited a school where they made much of the fact that there was a Director of Fun. Walking around the school it appeared that it was anything *but fun* to attend either as a student or member of staff. Apparently in the happy house 'it never rains' and to suggest otherwise is treasonous. If we all sing the refrain that everyone is happy then surely it will make it so. But it doesn't.

Happy House

A school's culture is heavily influenced by its leaders but everyone has an impact. As Vic Goddard tells heads, 'Remember we make the weather', but we are not the *only* people to shape the climate. Every single person in a school influences the mood of every other person, within a highly complicated web of emotion that shifts minute by minute. Sometimes one person can have a disproportionate impact on the whole ecosystem; senior leaders for instance, or that particularly naughty child or aggressive parent.

However, negativity seems to impact more than positivity which can be catastrophic for morale and individual wellbeing. It's the professional equivalent of doom-scrolling, not just feeling a bit fed up at work but going looking for reasons to be even more fed up. As leaders we have to acknowledge this and do our best to counter-balance it. Not through forced 'fun, fun, fun' or to 'pretend all's well' but by acknowledging when something is tough, or not working as it should. It's about being honest and working together to find a solution that is right for everyone. Sometimes it is simply not possible to remove the problem – consider the Covid lockdown as an example of that – but we can be proactive in our support of those struggling.

Getting on with your professional colleagues *should* be easy; you share common goals and face similar daily experiences after all. However, schools are also huge organisms with conflicting priorities, perceived hierarchies (not all subjects are created equal), different pay scales, never enough time and fragile egos. For those that work in schools, it is usually far more to us than just a job; it is a vocation, a calling, a duty and something we don't just clock-out of. Once, I worked as a cook in a hotel kitchen and I made a terrible lasagne, really sloppy and tasteless. The head chef told me in no uncertain terms that it was bloody awful, to throw it away and to start again. Fair enough, I thought, and did as I was told, not caring at all that my work had been trashed. However, every time someone points out something not quite working perfectly in one of my lessons or school it's like I've been punched in the stomach. My professional ego is dominated by a holier-than-thou sense that what I am doing is some of the most important work in the world and everything I do should be brilliant, or else I am an abject failure, and it is unacceptable to fail because my students are important. Leaders have to remember this when interacting with staff and this is what Vic means when he says we make the weather. Even when it is raining, don't pretend it's not raining, but be there with an umbrella.

Tribes

In most workplaces – and schools are not exempt – the staff body will divide into tribes. Sometimes it is by department (who has the most curriculum time, the best results, perceived to be the most important), by experience, length of service or by role. In all the schools I've worked for there have been three most noticeable divides. The first division is between core subjects and everyone else. Having been an English teacher, I was shocked when I taught a different subject at GCSE for a year and students would tell me it wasn't as important as English or maths and so hadn't revised or completed homework; I also had less curriculum time each week, so my one GCSE had half the time of the maths' one GCSE.

The second divide is between teachers and associate staff – and in some schools they are called non-teachers which is even more othering. Yet these are the people that properly run a school and keep it going: receptionists, admin, cleaners, caretakers, human resources, finance et al. I've observed teachers speak down to caretakers, which they have come to regret when they need help with a leaking window. Lastly, one of the largest divides can be between so-called curriculum and pastoral staff and this can happen at all levels, from deputy headteachers conflicted over curriculum pathways to teachers and pastoral colleagues falling out over who is responsible for a child's repeated poor behaviour.

Such tribal divides miss the point: we all have to work together to ensure the whole child is educated and safeguarded and that we all get the opportunity to fulfil our roles to the best of our abilities. The main barrier to smoother working is time and its impact on communication. Being able to sit down face to face and properly discuss concerns usually brings about a shared understanding and an agreed way forward. But too often it's a rushed corridor conversation when one or both colleagues are grumpy and in a rush, or a tersely worded email. As leaders we have to model that good communication: listen for meaning, not just to reply; hear what is said and what everyone's worries and fears are; reassure as much as possible; don't let your positional ego (I'm the boss) get in the way; and keep smiling. Ultimately leaders sometimes have to make unpopular decisions, but we do have control over how these are communicated.

Children's real homes

With regards to maintaining a happy house for students and their families, the protocol is the same. Take time to explain decisions and remember it is never personal, regardless of how it feels. Kids can say and do some awful things, particularly when scared or angry, and their parents are the same. Always remain calm and if you can't simply end the meeting and agree to come back to it later. There are occasions when this doesn't work out for you. Your school must have a policy in place for how to deal with threatening or aggressive parents or visitors in the same way as you have one for children. School leaders should protect colleagues from abuse, but that does not mean we simply suck it up ourselves. Maintain boundaries and stay calm. I have had to ban parents from site due to aggressive behaviour and also called the police when they have refused to leave. Being a punk leader does not mean head-butting anyone, even when they may deserve it.

For some children, their real homes are extremely unhappy and unsafe places. Occasionally these will become safeguarding disclosures and Early Help or Children's Services will become involved. All too often children living miserably fall just short of the threshold and these are the ones that dominate your thoughts: children whose parents dump them on relatives for weeks or even months at a time without explanation; parents that prioritise a new partner or new baby; children without enough to eat, no warmth, sleeping three to a bed.

As a leader you have some influence about what happens next – invitations to exciting days out and their costs covered, ensuring they get taken to a college or apprenticeship interview, simply providing a warm safe space with free lunches. Make sure you ensure something gets done; that does not mean you have to do it all yourself and you can't carry the worry around with you. Not because it doesn't matter, it does, but because it will burn you out and an awful lot of other children need you too.

Keeping Your Own House in Order

As a leader, how can you maintain a happy house when your own house is fairly miserable? Speaking as someone who has battled more than enough demons, some in my own mind and some dressed in an ill-fitting Marks and Spencer's suit, it is permissible to be a leader and experience emotions. Regardless of what anyone thinks, we're not robots existing in hermetically sealed happy suits, grinning relentlessly at everyone we see. We experience the whole range of human emotions and I do believe that the wider school community will appreciate your honesty so long as the negativity doesn't dominate.

I have tried to be honest with work colleagues at especially difficult periods of my life: post-partum depression, extreme anxiety when working for absolute knobs, the sudden illness of both parents, a bloody awful menopause. Regardless of how miserable I have felt on occasion I have always dragged myself in and I know chatting to great colleagues and amazing kids will raise my spirits. If that doesn't work I'll lock myself in my office; it is safer for everyone if I do this.

People understand. They come to me when they feel the same. They know they will not be judged. I'll do what I can to help but I'll never blandly tell them to just pull themselves together because that never works.

Punk leadership suggests

- Leaders make the weather, but everyone contributes to the climate; we must be proactive in ensuring we are as positive and sunny as possible.

- Don't create the false illusion of a happy house – schools are not all 'fun, fun, fun' – and to do so is disingenuous to your colleagues. Acknowledge where things can be improved.

- Staff bodies will fall into various tribes but that is OK so long as they don't fight against each other. Actively model that everyone is an equally valued colleague even though we all have different roles.

- Communication is the most important element of a happy workplace; it cannot be rushed, it should be face to face as much as possible and it should always be professional. If you're angry, don't press send on an email.

- Good communication with students and parents follows the same principles. But do not accept aggressive or abusive behaviour – challenge it appropriately and protect yourself and others.

5
Bad Dog
Managing Mistakes

Here's a Bitch Who'll Give it Back

God I love Chumbawamba. Well before 'Tubthumping' weirdly made them megastars and Danbert Nobacon poured water over John Prescott at the Brits, I'd spent many a happy evening seeing them live and have probably seen them live more than any other band. Their performances were anarchic, chaotic, creative, loud and bloody good fun. The era of *'Never Mind the Ballots*, *Shhh* and *Anarchy* is incredible, with the excellent 'English Rebel Songs 1381–1914' reminding us that punk goes back over seven centuries.

'Bad Dog' is one of my funeral songs. It's one of life's little pleasures to think of my mortal remains being carried towards a fiery pit accompanied by the fast-paced feminist rage of 'here's a bitch who will give it back'. The album from which it's taken, *Anarchy* was banned in some shops for its 'obscene' cover featuring the birth of a baby, the image actually taken from a children's book. The whole album is a fusion of punk, rave and angry politics. 'Bad Dog' articulates what it is like for women to be 'bitches' in a world where you are either a 'good girl, pat, pat' or a 'bad dog, smack, smack'. It resonates with all of us nasty women.

A Tale to Tell

I have made so many mistakes over the course of my career. Some have been relatively harmless, others make me squirm with embarrassment and a few still keep me awake at night. I know that it is not that common for leaders to own up to their mistakes; plenty of times I've witnessed blame being deflected or, worse, directed towards someone else. That's cowardice and arrogance. I really rate Steve Munby's book *Imperfect Leadership: A Book for Leaders Who Know They Don't Know It All*. All leadership is imperfect: we don't have all the answers, we can be distracted, and we will certainly make mistakes.

Teachers make a lot of mistakes. We try things in class that have no guarantee of working and that experimental approach is fine. I'm resistant to the idea that success is certain in a room of children; learning is too nebulous for that. I think occasionally you find an approach or a strategy more likely to work with most students, but it's never nailed on. And if children can be tricky, teachers are a bloody nightmare. Without a doubt I've made more mistakes with my colleagues than I have with my students and a few of them have never let me forget it.

Most mistakes, once the shame has subsided, make great anecdotes, particularly about the leadership journey itself. Like that time I accidentally sent an all-staff email suggesting we run a 'Dick of the Week' competition (lots self-nominated, a few were outraged, but we had badges ready to be won); or another all-staff email where I referred to a colleague as 'that hairy maths teacher'. Frankly, I made fewer mistakes when email wasn't a thing and you'd think I'd be better at recalling them by now.

We don't like to own up to our mistakes because that apportions blame and blame is frequently punished. No one much likes to be punished and perhaps one of the reasons I am more comfortable owning my mistakes now as a leader is that there are fewer people who will punish me. My colleagues are not my mum after all, and I've found that when I confess to my bosses they seem to view my confession as punishment enough especially if I've tried to make amends ('You said *what?*'). However, in an age where headteachers can be seen as more disposable than football managers, the consequences can be quite dire.

Sorry is the Hardest Word

If you start from the premise that everyone will make mistakes, life simply becomes easier all around. When you as a leader make a mistake, you have to own it, you have to articulate it and you have to do what you can to put it right. I learnt this in the classroom the hard way when I perhaps erroneously accused a child of a misdemeanour they were adamant they hadn't committed. I have seen some teachers dig their heels in even when faced with evidence to the contrary and it helps no one: a teacher who cannot bear to acknowledge they made a mistake and a child completely outraged that they've been accused of something they didn't do. A simple 'Sorry, I thought that was you talking but I was mistaken' can be far harder to say than it should be.

As the grown-ups in school, we simply must be better at saying sorry when we make a mistake. I have said sorry to classes for not marking papers as fast as I'd promised, for arriving late after being on duty, when I forgot to book the computer suite, and most often, 'I'm sorry, but yes this is English and we do have to do some reading and writing today.'

I have apologised to colleagues for being poorly organised and giving them a shorter deadline than I would like, for getting mixed up with dates, for having to move a parents' evening, and also for calling one of them a 'hairy maths teacher'.

The apologies I have had to make to parents and carers are rarely acknowledging one of my own personal mistakes, but these are perhaps more important. A little humility when needed goes a long way, especially if I can smooth things over for colleagues by taking one for the team. Occasionally leaders simply have to soak up the rage on behalf of someone else because we have broader shoulders (I am not talking about accepting abuse). I have apologised on behalf of colleagues because not enough homework was set as well as too much; because a teacher has lost that prohibited bracelet they've confiscated and because a receptionist slammed the phone down on someone swearing at her.

I've apologised to local residents for parents parking across their driveways and because Year 8 have had a water fight in the park on their way home on a hot day. I've even apologised to people because there is litter from the nearby chip shop outside the school gates, regardless of whether that is something we're responsible for or not.

But rarely are these apologies done to completely accept all blame for what has gone wrong. Sometimes the apology is simply an opening position to make it clear that we're here to discuss the real reason someone is upset. For example, it's not Year 8 having a water fight that is upsetting, rather it is them scattering plastic water bottles over people's lawns, shrieking so loudly it wakes babies and then scarpering. An apology at the start of a wider discussion can signal that you are shelving your ego to build a relationship.

Yes, it's possible to apologise too much, so much that the apologies become meaningless. I'm not proposing that every perceived slight earns a grovelling; we're not rugs to trample over, but I do think apology-avoidance at all costs is unhelpful.

Mistakes are Good

Good leaders actively help foster a creative, innovative culture in schools where children and their teachers try new things, regardless of whether they work as planned or not. Without a doubt these are not mistakes that require apologies. We know that children will only take risks if they are protected going into them and given a safe environment in which to fail. We have to make it clear that our classrooms are safe spaces to make those mistakes and it's OK to fail occasionally; not everyone passes their driving test the first time or gets 100% on every test; we've all been in relationships that have failed and slipped on the ice. Teachers have to create classrooms where if it doesn't work out then there is no shame, no blame, no punishment. Perfection is when their peers also don't judge them for having a go or when they don't do as well as others.

It is exactly the same for teachers. Teaching and learning is messy. Finding the right approach to maximise impact is always a process of trial and error, but in some schools this is being discouraged. Professionals are sticking to tried and tested approaches, even if there is a chance of improving, because of the risk. In some cases, the curriculum is delivered by rote with teachers becoming cookie-cutter deliverers of someone else's content. All creativity, innovation, excitement is abandoned; it's not fun and it's definitely not punk.

For the sake of sanity and workload you sometimes have to start with central-ised planning, a textbook, a worksheet or a website … but be a bit radical and adapt them for yourself as well as your learners even if you don't know what will happen next. That's where the magic lies.

Of course, what often prevents us from experimenting is that respon-sibility for when it doesn't work out and there *is* shame, blame and pun-ishment. Lessons are judged and graded, stern conversations are held that affect appraisal and performance-related pay. I've heard about schools where teachers are shouted at by managers, sometimes in front of students; belit-tled, ridiculed, bullied. When this is the culture of course you become risk-adverse because there is a bigger penalty for it going wrong than there is a reward for success.

Green Day's Billie Joe Armstrong said: 'Punk has always been about doing things your own way. What it represents for me is ultimate freedom and a sense of individuality.' Punk leaders can't be the only ones being creative and doing things their own way, they also have to foster a culture where both students and staff feel safe to take risks.

When Mistakes are Bad

Yeah, but sometimes things go *really badly*. Sometimes those mistakes in class-rooms are happening all day every day with no remedy. Sometimes what mas-querades as creativity is, in fact, chaos and nothing is learnt and no one is safe. These cases have to be addressed and challenged with compassion, patience, but a steely insistence that things must improve.

Occasionally there are incidents in school far more serious than a mistake even if it was not intentional. Several high-profile 'super heads' have ended up in prison because of heinous wrong doings ranging from fraud to sexual abuse. As a leader, and more so as a headteacher, there will be occasions when you come across something serious. These are distressing, alarming and troubling; they will make you angry or sad or simply confused.

This is not the time to go rogue because without a shadow of a doubt that will make it worse. There are always policies and procedures in place to follow and someone to report it to. There are plenty of sources of help to ensure you get it right, because if an allegation becomes an investigation every action you take will be later poured over. Getting the balance right is difficult, especially if the issue is emotive or personally triggering. Ensuring you don't jump to conclusions is essential; never brand children liars or believe everything without challenge. If a law has been potentially broken the matter must be referred to the police. Use the LADO (local authority designated officer).

These are some of the worst things to have to manage and the toll can be especially hard. A friend of mine had to manage some serious allegations of sexual abuse at her school, supporting both the family of the child making the allegations as well as the three members of staff named; families were shattered, careers damaged, and ultimately no action taken. She lost a week of her holiday with the police in school exploring locations, and the rest of the time was worried and stressed. Horrendous, but with the right support you get through it and later know you made a difference at the worst time of someone's life.

Punk leadership suggests

- That mistakes are inevitable and to be welcomed in the journey for improvement.
- When something goes wrong there is no shame in owning it; apologise without shame.
- Build cultures where mistakes are not feared and avoided.
- When something more serious happens take advice, follow the policy and refer on; you are not alone.

6
Monkey Gone to Heaven
Effective Line Management

Heaven

The first time I heard the Pixies I was visiting punk friends in an awful little bedsit and they were listening to *Doolittle*. 'I'm sorry', one apologised, 'I know they're American but I kind of like it', which sums up a certain attitude prevalent at the time: proper punk had to be musically coarse, lyrically harsh and definitely British; odd given where its roots were. No one ever said that about Iggy Pop or Lou Reed.

'Monkey Gone to Heaven' doesn't sound like an Eighties track; musically it feels much later and the lyrics reference environmentalism, the destruction of the planet and biblical numerology. I have wonderful memories of dancing to it with friends at *Snobs* in Birmingham in the late nineties and also of it being one of the few of my songs that my daughter liked, although I think she has grown out of this. To me it still sounds fresh and has only happy connotations.

Everything is Gonna Burn

If you get line management wrong pretty much everything can burn. It is an extremely important relationship that can often be left to chance without considering the personalities and the joint-journey needing to be travelled. Even worse is not guaranteeing protected and valuable time for the process to take place. As a head of department, I was line managed by the headteacher; the number of times I turned up for line management and simply had to stand outside in the corridor like a naughty student because he wasn't ready for me and something more important had cropped up. Once, line management took place in his car so we could talk while he drove around smoking a cigarette and got money out from a cash-point. No, I didn't feel very special although the vague hand gestures and his, 'You know what you're doing', was intended to make me feel confident.

Six

As a school leader you will be firmly wedged within a hierarchy, a proper line with those *below* you that you line manage and others *above* you that line manage you. Sometimes there are also colleagues alongside you, others of the *same rank* that you must engage with, and sometimes you will take the lead on something while at other times you will be led.

Of course, a linear hierarchy is an unhelpful shape in schools and most other large organisations; rather we are a messy jumbled-up web that is not purely based on your position within the organisation. I'm not sure why we are so obsessed with hierarchies except to massage egos and distribute blame. So *line* is the wrong word for the process that takes place but teachers are stubborn and even if I could think of something more appropriate they'd still call it *line* management regardless.

Even though I am currently the headteacher, I am still line managed by the Head of English when responsible for a class; if this class is in Years 7, 8 or 9 I am also line managed by the English KS3 Leader. I cannot hold them to account unless they are also quality assuring me, otherwise school improvement is something done *to* teachers and not with them. I am also accountable to the SENCO for meeting the needs of children with special educational needs and I need to ensure that I make the deadlines set for me by others. I can't simply say, *I don't feel like entering my class' progress data by your deadline because I am far too important, I'll do it when I want.*

Regardless of what type of line management I am engaging in, or with who, it is essential to establish the purpose and scope of the activity and create appropriate protected time for it. This is especially true if you are working alongside colleagues in a similar role. You may be one of several heads of department, of several Assistant or Deputy Headteachers and within Trusts there will be other Headteachers. Schools should be a dead zone for egos, for positional posturing but sadly they are not. However, if you want to work effectively with pretty much anyone but especially other *sixes* then it has to be in the true spirit of equity and collaboration.

This is easier said than done, particularly when your perception is that someone is making a pig's ear of something. An honest, frank but sensitive conversation is a good place to start. Too often we shy away from a direct conversation as the assumption is that it will be considered a confrontation. Understanding where someone is coming from is emotionally literate because honest and frank does not mean rude and upsetting. If that fails, there is usually someone further up that line you can discuss the matter with, either to gain some insight or talk through concerns. As long as these conversations are open and reasonable, and not bitching behind someone's back, it can be a useful coaching session. Learning how to work effectively with a huge variety of people is essential and you simply won't see eye to eye with everyone on your team.

Five

When you are line managing someone *below you* in the chain you must never behave as if they are *beneath you*. You are all professional colleagues and each of you will have different strengths, approaches, priorities and areas for development. The purpose of line management is usually really simple: to help that person be the best leader they can be in so they are effective in their role.

You do not have to be an expert in the area they are leading but some rudimentary knowledge in the right wheelhouse is more than useful. If you are line managing the Head of French, but you don't speak French let alone have taught it, you are still likely to have led a different type of department. Indeed, sometimes it is beneficial to be a few steps removed; I found line managing the Head of English really hard after I had moved on from this exact role. The poor middle leader had great ideas but it wasn't the way I would have done it. Being able to stand back and not just expect others to mimic your leadership can be challenging.

Curriculum design, analysing student performance and agreeing necessary steps to improve it, confirming suitable improvement priorities applying school policies equitably and consistently and dealing with paperwork are all fairly straightforward. What takes the time and skill is managing people. Getting a team of adults in schools all going in the same direction at the same time can be nigh on impossible. When you line manage a middle leader it's not even your group of people that need managing, it is theirs; your role is to help them do it without taking over and so they become more skilled and confident in this.

One of the hardest elements of this is many leaders' role as player-manager; they are still on the pitch playing whilst also being the person in charge. Occasionally the leader will have come up the ranks and that transition from being part of the team to leading it can be really tricky. One day you're moaning about leadership in the staffroom and suddenly you've moved to the dark side. The colleagues you now have to manage may have seen you struggle with classes, make mistakes or even get tipsy on nights out. It can be extremely difficult to maintain friendships but it is not impossible. If you don't like the idea that you may have to discuss performance with someone, or investigate a parental complaint, then do consider seeking promotion in a different setting.

Seven

Line management also goes upwards; everyone is accountable to someone. As a headteacher I am line managed by the Trust CEO but also accountable to the Chair of Governors. My CEO is line managed by the Chair of the trustees. At various points we are all accountable to governors, trustees, the Department for Education – regionally and nationally – Local Authorities as well as staff, students, parents, carers and the wider community. Line management is not a line, and even if it was the line does not stop with one person.

Managing upwards is a genuine skill as it works best if your boss doesn't realise that's what you're doing. It might be something as simple as reminding them about when your meetings are (regardless of Outlook invites), insisting that this time is protected and valued and being relentless with prioritising your priorities. It might be the constant gentle nudge about funding or staffing changes or adaptions to policy and practice. Often it is providing an accurate evaluation of your team because you know them best. For example, if a learning walk has not gone particularly well it is crucial that you are insistent about what the bigger picture is, how this one snapshot differs from ongoing quality assurance (and the opposite is also true).

You are in partnership with the person that line manages you although it's entirely possible that you don't particularly like them. Liking someone is not a prerequisite for professional collaboration although it can help. Seek their advice and support and work to build trust and positive rapport. And if that isn't possible just bloody leave.

Keeping the Band Playing

Any school department, including the senior leadership team, is essentially a band. You have a common purpose, whether that is making music or delivering high-quality education to children. You should have the same vision, values and goals, which could be creating punk or hip-hop or folk, and in schools this will tend to be a natty slogan which hopefully is lived rather than simply laminated. But everyone in a band has a different role and every band has a different composition; UB40 is very different in shape to ZZ Top. Not everyone can be the guitarist and it is entirely possible that you may covet someone else's position. After all, Dave Grohl was Nirvana's drummer but guitarist and singer for Foo Fighters. Similarly, you may start in one role and move on to another either by design or happenchance. This is an essential element of punk leadership.

What matters is that the band keeps playing because everyone else on stage or in the audience needs the song to continue. Music history is littered with occasions where a band member has stormed off stage in the middle of a performance and punk certainly has its fair share of tantrums. After all, one of punk's most iconic images is The Clash's Paul Simonon smashing up his bass live on stage. Frankly, if it matters, if you are bothered about it, passions will run high.

Choose your team wisely, either the one you join or the one you put together, because on occasion the team will become a line and it still must function.

The Monkey

Someone has a problem; this is the monkey. The monkey is loud, time-consuming, messy and no one actually wants to keep hold of it. Someone brings the monkey to you; they say they want to discuss it – but really what they want is for you to take the monkey off them. Their plan is to leave your office with the monkey firmly on your desk to cause havoc. The monkey bringer could be *anyone*. It could be your boss, your colleague, someone you line manage; it doesn't matter because *you do not want that monkey*.

You not only need to find a way to ensure they leave with their own monkey, but ideally they take an extra one of yours as well. Not only does this make your desk lighter, it is far less likely they'll bring a monkey to you ever again.

I do know some colleagues who accept so many monkeys they might as well open a zoo. They're famous for it because they can't say no. And why would they say no when saying *yes* means alleviating someone else's workload or anxiety, ensuring work is done right or that students are not disadvantaged?

When I was one of two Deputy Headteachers my counterpart would come to me with a grin and say, 'I have a monkey for you … give me one of yours' and this was fine, we worked in tandem to manage the zoo – and that is great teamwork.

Punk leadership suggests

....

- True school line management is not linear, it is far messier and always fluid so never consider your position in the perceived hierarchy as unassailable. If you're bothered by taking instructions from someone competent in a less advanced role then you need to shelve your ego.

- Every team member has different skills, strengths and purposes; use that to the benefit of the whole school or wider organisation. You simply don't have to like everyone to make great music together.

- Don't unfairly dump your monkeys on other people, and certainly never accept more monkeys than you can reasonably manage; they can be vicious little blighters.

7
No More Heroes

Tackling Work–Home Balance

Formed in the mid to late 1970s, The Stranglers became one of the most successful early punk bands with anthems like 'No More Heroes' and 'Peaches'. They faced criticism around allegedly racist and sexist lyrics, which they countered by saying it was ironic and satire. Certainly, I feel extremely uncomfortable with the lyrics to 'Peaches' irony or not.

'No More Heroes' seems to lament how there are no more strong heroes in popular culture. However, the heroes named – Trotsky, Lenin, Elmyra, Sancho Panza – were all either murdered by former devotees or got to watch 'their Rome burn'. So, what is in it for the heroes themselves except death, despair and witnessing the destruction of all they created?

Bassist Jean-Jacques Burnel was quoted as saying, 'I thought of myself as part of punk at the time because we were inhabiting the same flora and fauna … I would like to think The Stranglers were more punk plus and then some.'[1]

I'm not sure what 'punk plus' means – better? Different? Intelligent? The Stranglers have been accused of a little arrogance but most people who put themselves up on a stage can come across as that.

Heroes

We all love to be a bit of a hero, yes? Education lends itself to individuals committed to making a difference, changing lives for the better and merging professional identities with the personal. It can sometimes make us unpopular with other professionals who do not see their line of work as a deep vocation, as something that dominates their life. I remember being in a pub with a rather enthusiastic newly qualified teacher who was explaining to someone not in education that teaching was who they were, it was part of them; I noted the cynicism and disdain, the laughing behind her back. The teacher's earnestness may have been a *Dead Poet's Society* sentiment but it is not usual in every line of work. It's sort of 'work plus'.

I have to confess that I do consider teaching to be a part of who I am and not just a job that I do. Occasionally, I might have been evangelical about this, virtue signalling my commitment and sacrifice to all who would listen. At other times I have resented it – when not being able to separate personality and job has caused pain, stress, anxiety and an inability to manage workload. So many teachers (and I know this is not limited to education) will dream about leaving the classroom forever so that at the end of the day the work is done, left behind, thought of no more. But of course, we never do, we simply have to get better at managing it.

Of course, the way that we perceive what is required to be a dedicated teacher seems to become more intense as a leader. As a classroom teacher your responsibility is for the thirty children in front of you; as you become a leader it becomes every child. There has to be a correlation between the scope of your responsibilities and how this impacts your sense of being. It certainly impacts your stress, anxieties and workload. A retiring CEO, former headteacher and chair of the Headteachers' Roundtable wrote in his blog, 'It Wasn't the Hours I Worked it Was the Hours I Worried.'[2]

Rome is Burning

A 2018 article in *The Guardian*[3] titled, 'Do you work more than 39 hours a week? Your job could be killing you' explored the health impact of excessive workloads in all professions. There has become an expectation that 'lunch is for wimps'[4] for far too many of us. I know of no full-time teacher or leader working less than 39 hours, despite what some would have you believe about the contractual 1265 hours a year. Even worse, I know of some people who go down to four days a week so they can have a whole day to catch up on work – unpaid.

We all know it's shocking but too often it is seen as a badge of honour, of being a hero. That is what the job is, what it's always been and the kids are too important not to do it for. We end up embedding this sacrificial culture into our leadership as well: not only do we often work harder as leaders but we can expect our teams to work harder too – because that's what we did when we were in that position. Home working during Covid has exacerbated this further; it's become increasingly normalised.

Even before the pandemic, teachers were paid substantially less per hour worked than other professionals. It has been suggested[5] through a trade union analysis of official data that teachers in England work over 12 unpaid hours per week, which is more than any other job (Millions of workers doing unpaid overtime, research shows, The *Independent*). All too frequently the response is to tut, nod, but not think anything can be done.

And what's the result? We are watching our Rome burn: high absence rates for staff who have worse physical and mental health than ever before and a recruitment and retention crisis beyond anything previously seen. In the 2022/23 year, the Government's own statistics[6] show that 93% of the initial teacher training recruitment target was met in primary (down from 131% the year before) and only 59% in secondary (down from 79%). Although recruitment to Initial teacher training (ITT) increased during the pandemic, these statistics do not reveal how many completed training, made it to the classroom or are still there.

A March 2023 article in *The Guardian*[7] cited that teacher vacancies were up 93% and vacancies in schools were up by 37%. Teachers seem to be moving between schools and also completely leaving the classroom. One of the biggest demographics of teachers leaving is women in their thirties, often corresponding to when they are starting families.

By the time we become leaders, where the workload and pressures deepen, it is simply an accepted reality. But it doesn't have to be; as leaders we are precisely in the right position to smash it up a bit and find a better path. We may not have sufficient school funding to move to having half a teacher's timetable dedicated to 50% PPA (planning, preparing and assessment) but there are other things we can do.

Firstly, what is really important in your school? What improves the quality of teaching and learning? How do we ensure all are safeguarded? Then focus *just* on that.

Teachers need to build effective relationships to know the children that they teach, any specific learning needs and how to teach them effectively. They need to understand every nuance of their curriculum. From this they need to plan appropriate lessons, teach them and then provide feedback and next steps in learning. Along the way all children must be safeguarded so teachers have to know what signs to look for and then what to do if there is a disclosure or concern. And that's about it.

Sure, we want them to change lives, be inspirational and creative, but that doesn't really impact on time. And although it would be lovely for all lessons to be planned and resourced from scratch, laminated and pretty, it isn't crucial. Shared base-planning can be your friend so long as it is carefully crafted around the needs of your children and the specifics of your curriculum. It then has to be adapted for your own class as one size really doesn't fit all. Planning by download rarely saves time in the long run; planning not designed for your own context and class won't fit very well, and the lesson may not go to plan, which causes additional stress about behaviour and lost learning as well as picking up the pieces afterwards.

Schools following a centralised curriculum and using centralised resources may seem tempting when faced with workload concerns as well as quality of provision. However, if our wonderful teaching profession is being boiled down to plug-and-play facilitators at the front of the room, you no longer need highly skilled and trained teachers. You need facilitators and these are both considerably less bothersome to recruit and train and much cheaper to employ.

Therefore, punk leaders will encourage some shared base-planning but we will also ensure you have the space to plan, prepare and assess properly by giving you as much time as we can afford and making sure we're not loading loads of silly extras on you. Being in control of your classroom, being trusted to use your professional judgement and being supported to do so is what alleviates stress. Exhaustion, no – but you will fall asleep contented and professionally sated. Punk leaders will actively look to cut out what is not necessary or important; they will prioritize actions and support people and teams to do their best without demoralising them or pretty much killing them off.

And although some leaders are great at this, *for others* they are not always good at doing it for themselves. Leadership is a step up in responsibility but that does not need to come with the expectation that you work every hour to the exclusion of everything else. Again, it is about not being a martyr because the best leaders model expectations to others, including workload. Not long ago a senior leadership job advert was shared on social media in which the head had rather misjudged the room through a very forthright description of the expectation that to work at that school candidates would be in early, go home late, have no breaks and slog over the weekend. Some ridiculed it, some thought that the advert was at least being honest and these were the expectations for senior leaders. But that is simply not the case.

We can all learn to be more judicious in our use of time and the tasks we undertake. Sure, laminating and then double-bordering those vision statements make them pretty, but will this seriously improve your school or the children's learning? Dragging yourself in with a migraine because of a misaligned sense of presenteeism is only likely to make your health worse and everyone around you nervous.

Shakespearoes

When Shakespeare wanted to use a word that didn't exist he made it up; thus the dictionary is bountiful with his wonderful vocabulary. Similarly, The Stranglers made up the word Shakespearoes, which some adore but most detest.

Punk leaders need to create their own workload lexicon for themselves and for their teams. It has to be modelled, articulated and openly allowed. All the time I have been a headteacher I have also been a mum; for many working in education there is a motherhood penalty where you are treated differently after you become a parent: less money, fewer promotional opportunities, guilt-tripped around availability. Because of this I have always deliberately emphasised how I am making being both mum and headteacher work and that others may not do it my way but it's OK to pioneer their own route.

Sometimes I have to leave right on the bell. I tell people I am leaving right on the bell and why. Perhaps my daughter has a medical appointment, perhaps it's because I've not spent time with her much recently and I need to remind her who

I am. I make it very explicit that no one should routinely be sending emails over the weekends or between 7:00pm to 7:00am (sure, write them but delay sending) and even better, take that app off your phone. I ensure the deadlines I give are suitable, causing no one to panic and always achievable; usually everything is published at the start of the year and changes minimised. I have to keep saying this aloud to everyone because unless it is repeated no one quite believes it; it takes a long time to change embedded behaviour.

And then the hardest thing is making others stick to it: middle and senior leaders are really good at sneaking loads of extra things in without you spotting it – emails at 8:00pm on a Sunday evening requiring a turnaround for Monday morning are the worst; no wonder there is so much Sunday night dread. As a profession we have allowed ourselves to normalise extraordinarily harmful behaviours, pretty much whacking an ice pick into our own brain. It must stop.

Punk leadership suggests

- Teaching does not need more heroes; do not sacrifice your happiness, health and wellbeing because it is an important vocation.
- Use your time judiciously but remember you are a highly trained and skilled teacher, not a plug-and-play automaton.
- Leaders must facilitate sufficient time and space for teachers to plan, prepare and assess without becoming overwhelmed or burnt out.
- Leaders have to openly and consistently model healthy balanced approaches to work, reinforcing those expectations with other leaders. We are heroes but let's not watch our Rome burn.

Notes

1 Punk77 (n.d.) *JJ Burnel Stranglers Interview Pt2 – Punk Rock*. [online] Available at: http://www.punk77.co.uk/groups/stranglersjjburnelin052.htm [Accessed 29 Jan. 2024].

2 LeadingLearner (2014) *Learning to Live with Leadership*. [online] @LeadingLearner. Available at: https://leadinglearner.me/2014/04/05/learning-to-live-with-leadership/ [Accessed 29 Jan. 2024].

3 Fleming, P. (2018) Do you work more than 39 hours a week? Your job could be killing you. [online] *The Guardian*. Available at: https://www.theguardian.com/lifeand-style/2018/jan/15/is-28-hours-ideal-working-week-for-healthy-life [Accessed 29 Jan. 2024].

4 *Wall Street* (dir. Oliver Stone, 1987).

5 World Education Blog (2021) *There is wide disparity in teachers' working hours.* [online] Available at: https://world-education-blog.org/2021/01/07/there-is-wide-disparity-in-teachers-working-hours/ [Accessed 29 Jan. 2024].

6 Department for Education (2023) Initial Teacher Training Census, Academic Year 2021/22. [online] Available at: https://explore-education-statistics.service.gov.uk/find-statistics/initial-teacher-training-census [Accessed 29 Jan. 2024].

7 Weale, S. (2023) *Teacher vacancies in England 93% higher than pre-pandemic, study finds.* The Guardian. [online] 23 March. Available at: https://www.theguardian.com/education/2023/mar/23/teacher-vacancies-in-england-93-higher-than-pre-pandemic-study-finds [Accessed 29 Jan. 2024].

8
Should I Stay or Should I Go?

Recruitment and Retention

The Rubber Bishops

In the early nineties I got to see comedy duo The Rubber Bishops perform a few times. Bill Bailey and Martin Stubbs dressed as youth-wing bishops, 'Putting the suss back into Jesus', and performed bastardised versions of popular tunes. I have no idea what happened to Martin but Bill continued to make music, be funny, take a keen interest in wildlife and got quite good at dancing. The first time I saw them, they performed 'Should I Stay or Should I Go?' as 'Should I Spit or Should I Swallow?' I laughed so hard snakebite and black came out of my nose.

'Should I Stay or Should I Go?' remains The Clash's only number 1 single in the UK and that was a good decade after it was originally released. Punks don't really strive to be in the top ten; it's not about the popularity and the commercial success, it's about the music. When speaking in 1991, Mick Jones said of the song, 'We were just playing, that was the kind of thing we used to like to play.'[1]

Say that You are Mine

Perhaps if working in schools was all about just getting on with the job, loving what you do and performing for the kids rather than trying to get into the top ten there would be less of a recruitment and retention crisis. I have explored some key school themes in earlier chapters and although I don't want to repeat myself it is worth pouring some of the sector's greatest concerns into the recruitment and retention powder keg.

Without a doubt we are not retaining a significant proportion of the people that at some point have chosen to work in schools. We're not keeping heads, leaders, teachers or associate staff and the attrition rate is worsening. You have only to read Headrest's Annual Wellbeing Report 2023[2] where they identify a range of stressors including, 'burnout, moral injury, recruitment, workload (small schools especially), budget, and of course, the ubiquitous Ofsted and it's [sic] pernicious approach to unintelligent accountability'. And at the time of writing the impact of headteacher Ruth Perry's death is still very much felt, along with news articles such as *The Guardian*'s in March 2023 headlined: 'Revealed: stress of Ofsted inspections cited as factor in deaths of 10 teachers.'[3]

Sadly, in many schools these stresses trickle down; often by accident and occasionally by design in schools where senior leaders are determined to point the finger at anyone other than themselves when things do not go well. I truly believe that the vast majority of schools and trusts are led by good people who care for all in their community. However, I also know for a fact that there some terribly toxic schools. On occasion I have found myself in one, either working there or visiting. Of course, no one flourishes under an Orwellian regime. We forget that we can walk away and a massive benefit of a recruitment and retention crisis is that staff become valuable commodities to keep. I am aware that some schools behave appallingly to keep staff: the threat of a terrible reference, refusing to allow time out of school for interviews and even alluding to disciplinary or capability proceedings.

But it is simple: walk away and sort the mess out later; do not be scared to do this because the toll on your health, happiness, career and family can be horrendous if you are bullied into staying. Twice I have walked away, both times I was the 'major bread winner' with a dependent child, a mortgage and plenty of bills to pay. Both times I ended up landing on my feet. I know many people who have walked away, a few that have run, and none of them regret it. So be brave; you get to say which place of work you belong to.

End of Time

For the majority of schools the greatest resource is their staff: invest in them, train them, treat them with dignity and respect and you might well keep them until the end of time. In terms of practical strategies to retain great staff, with any decision to stay or go there are pull and push factors and leaders should focus on enhancing the pulls and minimising the pushes for their own institution. That's not a simple algorithm to run, you have to know your school, your staff and consider the priorities.

Some of the most frequent pull factors cited in many staff surveys are feeling trusted to do your job and having a good relationship with your immediate line manager. These are good places to start, so how can you develop this culture in your school? Being a great leader of people is not something that comes naturally to everyone, it has to be developed through training, not just left to chance. Often people are promoted to leadership posts because they are pretty good at the job they are currently doing but there is no guarantee they'll be as successful in the next one. Appropriate, kind, enabling, skilful and mature leadership takes time and we never stop learning. We can't all be Sarina Wiegman overnight.

A proper induction to any leadership post has to be accompanied by quality mentoring and coaching. For that reason in Headrest's Annual Report 2023 one of their seven recommendations is to, 'Ensure a fully funded induction and mentoring programme for all new headteachers and for those appointed from September 2019.'[4] That mentoring needs to be extended to all newly appointed leaders, not just heads.

On My Knees

Even in the most nurturing of schools we sometimes feel on our knees. Teaching is physically and emotionally demanding at the very best of times. During and post pandemic is not the best of times; I've never known it so bloody hard. More than ever, I have seen really inspirational and committed people down tools and leave the profession entirely: early retirement, establishing a tattoo studio, opening a café, investing in a carpet and upholstery cleaning business and a few teaching assistants are earning better money and working more convenient hours at the local supermarket.

It's not just about workload. It's about a rise in significant mental health issues for staff as well as students and their families, which in turn has fed a decline in behaviour and attendance. Doing the job in and out of the classroom is just hard graft and often little fun. Being laid bare by Ofsted, by league tables, by clickbait articles in local newspapers, shouting threatening parents in Reception and libellous assertions on social media makes it much worse, even in schools where staff are cherished. These are stressors that cannot be managed by anyone in a school, it is the responsibility of government, of social media companies and local paper editors to act protectively of a profession under siege; and that looks unlikely at the moment. Without those interventions the built-up anger in local communities simply feels justified to those shouting; that parent in Reception is probably not even angry at the school; schools remain one of the few places people have direct access to. When you are angry at the world about rising living costs, access to health care or landlords evicting you, it is school that remains open and accessible.

Whom I'm Supposed to be

When the government is repeatedly missing its targets for teacher training, sometimes you just have to take matters into your own hands. There are potentially thousands of individuals that would make amazing teachers or pastoral support but think it is too late. For many, going to university was simply not a perceived option and there were too many barriers: family expectations, low attainment when in school, the need to contribute financially, having a family early, and so on. For those with degrees they might have started in a different line of work but cannot now afford a pay cut to start training. I've seen so many ponderings on social media from people in their thirties, forties, fifties, bemoaning having left it too late. It should never be too late.

At my school we are growing our own staff: looking for potential and aptitude and finding affordable routes into the profession. Our Science Technician was always incredible when he popped into classrooms; at a time when supply teaching in science was high he stepped in and the kids loved it. He had a passion for the subject, incredible relationships with young people and a clear way of explaining what they needed to know and understand. But he didn't have a degree. So now we are helping him finance a part-time degree whilst employing him as an unqualified teacher and supporting with additional professional learning in school. Similarly we have supported a former teaching assistant gain an English degree and she is now a qualified teacher.

I am also optimistic about proposed (at the time of writing) undergraduate teacher apprenticeships. Writing in *Schools Week* in support of them, Professor Sam Twiselton acknowledges concerns 'in the sector about the potential for this to undermine the profession'.[5] No pathway into teaching which guarantees more graduates teaching, regardless of their route, can be a bad thing. The profession will be undermined if teaching adopts a doctor-nurse approach whereby qualified teachers plan and unqualified facilitators are in the classroom; and it will definitely be undermined if our empty classrooms are filled by substandard supply.

Indecision's Bugging Me

Plenty of times during my thirty-year long career in education I have seriously considered leaving. I have moved on from schools because they were not good fits, because I felt ill-treated by leaders or because the time was ripe for me to take the next step. Possibly five times I have considered quitting completely. Nail technician, a little café on the Welsh coast, painter and decorator, member of parliament, an animal sanctuary abroad, poet living in a cottage with cats on a cliff ... all pipedreams and never truly enacted.

What has kept me in the classroom and in the profession even at the toughest of times has been my commitment to improving the lives of young people. It has been the fun you can have in the classroom teaching the most amazing, revolutionary things. It's been results days, proms, getting name-checked or gushed at by former students. It's even the most heart-breaking of days when a child makes a disclosure to you, or you lose one of the community yet everyone pulls together. The camaraderie in one school can be multiplied a hundred times over in the wider teaching profession. We are a tribe and I feel like I belong here.

To recruit and retain the best staff in the future it is that culture of contribution and belonging that must be fostered in our own schools by leaders and in the wider community by those responsible for how we are treated and presented. We will never not need inspirational and skilled teachers.

Punk leadership suggests

- We have a recruitment and retention crisis; the solution is always revolutionary and it's time for the sector to lead the way.

- Recruiting into the profession will only happen through providing diverse and unusual routes into classrooms; grow your own teachers, associate staff and leaders. Invest.

- Retain by creating a climate where everyone feels trusted, valued and contributes. This is not a natural skill for some people but can be developed through coaching and mentoring.

- You have to know when it's time to move on – and also when to stay. Sometimes being happier at work is more important than a *better* title or salary.

Notes

1   The Clash (1991) *Clash on Broadway* box set liner notes (Media notes), Sony.
2   Headrest (2023) *2023 Annual Headteacher Wellbeing Report*. [online] Available at: https://www.headrestuk.co.uk/blog/headteacher-wellbeing-report-2023 [Accessed 29 Jan. 2024].
3   Fazackerley, A. (2023) *Revealed: Stress of Ofsted Inspections Cited as Factor in Deaths of 10 Teachers*. The Observer. [online] 25 March. Available at: https://www.theguardian.com/education/2023/mar/25/revealed-stress-of-ofsted-inspections-cited-as-factor-in-deaths-of-10-teachers [Accessed 29 Jan. 2024].

4   Headrest (2023) *2023 Annual Headteacher Wellbeing Report.* [online] Available at: https://www.headrestuk.co.uk/blog/headteacher-wellbeing-report-2023 [Accessed 29 Jan. 2024].

5   Twiselton, S. (2023) *Teacher Apprenticeships: A Policy We Should All Welcome.* [online] schoolsweek.co.uk. Available at: https://schoolsweek.co.uk/why-we-should-welcome-undergraduate-teacher-apprenticeships/ [Accessed 29 Jan. 2024].

9
Teenage Kicks

An Engaging and Relevant Curriculum

APeeling

The Undertones, possibly Derry's only punk band, were breaking up in 1978 when 'Teenage Kicks' was released. The band themselves did not count it as one of their best songs despite the incredible impact of having the song repeatedly played by John Peel on his influential Radio 1 show. It remained one of Peel's favourite tracks and was the last song played at his funeral.

The back of the cover to 'Teenage Kicks' features the Derry graffiti: *Undertones – shit, pish, counts, wankers*. If nothing else, it perhaps emphasises the need for correct spelling when communicating insults.

Influenced by The Ramones' simple chords and pounding drums, 'Teenage Kicks' has become a punk classic that has been adopted by other musical tribes; even my dad loves it. It is hard not to pump a fist and sing along, despite what that Derry graffiti might have intimated.

The Battleground

Ironically just as punk was being born in 1976, then Prime Minister James Callaghan delivered a speech at Ruskin College that, in the words of Andrew Adonis thirty years later, 'lit a flare that has illuminated education reform ever since'.[1] It stimulated a debate about the purpose of education and whether there should be 'a basic curriculum with universal standards'.[2]

In 1988 the first statutory National Curriculum was introduced by Secretary of State for Education Ken Baker with the first teaching of it starting in 1989. I trained as a teacher in 1994–95, just as Ron Dearing was leading a review into slimming it down. The current 2014 edition is more of a pamphlet than the original heavy tomes but still identifies prescribed subjects and content for children in England aged 5 to 16. Although there are many ways to avoid the National Curriculum, such as being an Academy or an independent school, the vast majority of schools adhere to the core content and principles, mostly to keep the inspectorate happy.

Without a doubt, the curriculum has become a messy battleground, akin to the Great War's no man's land, with opposing sides firmly entrenched and firing shots at each other; no one really wins. The division is largely arbitrary, and I wonder if it is a peculiarly British thing, to bunker down as either a *Traditionalist* or *Progressive* and spend hours on Twitter slagging one another off. It is certainly not as romantic as a Mod v Rocker Brighton Beach riot or even Montagues v Capulets slain on the streets of Verona. It is tiresome and rarely improves anything for children.

A traditional curriculum appears to be what my dad was taught in the 1950s. His strongest memories of school were undoubtedly extracurricular, including the glee of successfully adding pink sheep-dip dye to the school's water tank. He can also still recite most of Tennyson's *The Charge of the Light Brigade* by heart, and frequently does so at Christmas.

Conversely, a progressive curriculum seems to be what my mum was being taught at the same time. Mum attended Bath School of Art between the ages of 11 and 16; funded by the local authority, it appears to have been an early Studio School. She was taught English, maths, science, history, geography, and the like through the medium of art and design. Her father, my grandad, would have been a revolutionary punk had he not been a bit of a *Daily Mail*-reading Tory. He was traditional in every possible way except that he wanted an exclusively progressive, creative and innovative education for his daughter.

Both my parents are intelligent people who have made good lives for themselves and provided materially and lovingly for their children despite not moving on to further education; I came along when they were barely out of their teenage years. Both my parents *enjoyed* their school experience though; their experience of school has been far more important than the qualifications they obtained, and they have continued to be committed to learning new things, reading vociferously and being passionate about things important to them.

I suppose an interesting starting point for curriculum design is *what is the purpose of education?* However, I maintain that there is no absolute answer to such a question and to attempt one ultimately reduces the beauty and power of learning down to a few glib and controversial soundbites. Learning and education are at the centre of everything about life; it evolves, it is personal, it is wonderful and it equips for life; it happens in the classroom but also in corridors, the playground, the streets, importantly at home and increasingly online.

In a profession that can become far too entrenched in separate camps, pragmatists know that you need a little of everything to work. Children learning important knowledge and facts is essential but not at the expense of exploration, discovery and mastery of skills. Yes, I want my cake *and* I want to eat it.

Botheredness

Crucially, for schools to be truly great everyone has to be bothered about the curriculum. Teachers need to be invested in what they are teaching, and children need to care about it so that they become absorbed by it.

Botheredness is a fantastic word and was coined by travelling teacher and educationalist Hywel Roberts. If you have not explored his books *Botheredness* (2023), *Oops! Helping Children Learn Accidentally* (2012) and, with Debra Kidd, *Uncharted Territories: Adventures in Learning* (2018) please do so; they're awesome. He also brews a mean *Jolly Boys* pint.

I will not paraphrase Hywel here as I would not do him justice, but regardless of whether you have an uber-trad knowledge-intense curriculum or a dynamically progressive skills-based one, children need to genuinely care about what they are learning to do it justice; for that to happen their teachers have to care.

Teachers care about a curriculum that they help design, plan and polish even if they have to remain within broad guidelines. Part of being a professional teacher is having the skills and knowledge to consider the needs of your young people and create something suitable that will really grab their attention. But we are not entertainers, we're not Noel Edmonds are we?

After all, my mum's arty-farty education in the sixties led her to a lifetime of wanting to learn new things: she became a champion goat breeder, an agricultural show organiser, a maker of weird German dried flower hats; she cornered the market in used but unfranked stamps and became brilliant at patchwork, tapestry, knitting, stained glass and glass-fusing.

As explored elsewhere in this book, I am vehemently opposed to the homogenisation of the teaching profession, and this especially extends to curriculum design. A curriculum designed by specialists in the relevant age range, phase and subject, who work with those children, meeting the needs of those children, is vastly preferable to something formulated remotely and sent over to implement uniformly. As a secondary English specialist you'd be bonkers to put me in charge of an Early Years curriculum. I am not impervious to the occasional need to have something *oven-ready*, for example if a school cannot recruit in a particular area, but there has been a worrying trend in some multi-academy trusts to have a trust-approved curriculum. This might be great fun for those writing it, and surely gives the illusion of compliance and consistency, but it is truly soulless and there are better solutions.

Knowledge

Knowledge is OK, you know? Knowledge is the wrong battlefield because we all need to *know* things but we also need to *understand* those things, be *critical* of them as well as being able to *do* things. For some, knowledge became everything, a sort of pub quiz curriculum where there is tons and tons to remember, so much it hurts the brain and alienates a good many, just to be regurgitated in exams where everything has to be remembered. It is not possible for most, especially if you're not that bothered about it.

But knowledge itself is never a problem; knowledge matters, it is important, particularly in an age when every fact is up for debate and interpretation. No, I will not agree to differ with you on whether the Earth is flat.

Who determines the *right* knowledge is hugely problematic; the British trivium has been largely devised by white middle-class Christian men (and although I'm British, that trivium is mainly English). The required wholesale changes required become mild *woke* tinkerings around the edges. It is remarkable how often the very best of thought and culture tends to be West European in origin. Some may argue that this is Britain, dominated by British people with a British history and culture even if many other communities now call this home. It is undoubtedly imperialist and colonial. However, the world has changed, for young people there are no borders as their experience is often online. They are coming into contact and becoming friendly with people from all over the world, and this is a fantastic, enriching opportunity. When I went to school, I had a French pen pal. It didn't make my French any better and once we'd sent a couple of letters to each other about pets and hobbies it fizzled out. We welcomed a German exchange student into our home when I was 14; that was more useful as we could hold proper conversations and we shared an interest in punk. When she went home it again fizzled out. Now, these friendships across the world are far more consistent and definitely more varied. I will not brush over the safeguarding concerns about online friendships, but when conducted safely they are liberating. Therefore, a narrow jingoistic curriculum becomes increasingly exposed to a generation learning different content elsewhere. We need to keep up.

The *Animal Farm* Curriculum

All subjects are equal but some are more equal than others.

Of course, we all want an inclusive, diverse curriculum where students explore the humanities, sciences, literature, sports and the arts. We want children to master a musical instrument as well as algebra. To know the periodic table whilst singing opera. But we're not going to measure a school's success that way; which in turn will severely alter the curriculum that is offered, the experience children have and the professionals that are employed.

Yes, I am talking about the English Baccalaureate, a measure arbitrary but pernicious, designed to ensure children are *encouraged* to choose two of the following at GCSE: history, geography, computer science and a modern foreign language. And when I say modern foreign language I of course include Classic Greek and Biblical Hebrew.[3]

At many secondary schools students are now no longer given a choice of Key Stage 4 options. They *have* to choose two EBacc subjects to demonstrate a broad and balanced curriculum regardless of skill, interest or need. Subjects such as music, art, drama, design technology, religious studies, social sciences, vocational subjects, they all become less necessary, less important, and the children know it. And a limited curriculum limits our children and the entire country.

Punk leadership suggests

....

- The best curriculum is created by passionate and skilled professionals who design something aspirational for the children they know. Everyone has to be bothered about the curriculum for it to work: children, teachers, parents and the communities they are part of.
- The *Trad* and *Prog* dichotomy is apocryphal and, frankly, bollocks.
- Knowledge is absolutely fundamental – but who is choosing that knowledge and how is it chosen?
- It is time for a curriculum revolution: smash it up and start again; we need to encourage a love of learning in a world with few borders.
- Encourage kids to learn for kicks.

Notes

1 The Guardian (2006) *30 years on, Callaghan's words resonate.* [online] Available at: https://www.theguardian.com/politics/2006/oct/17/education.schools [Accessed 29 Jan. 2024].

2 Gillard, D. (2010) *Jim Callaghan – Ruskin College speech* (1976). [online] Available at: http://www.educationengland.org.uk/documents/speeches/1976ruskin.html [Accessed 29 Jan. 2024].

3 Department for Education (2023) *English Baccalaureate: eligible qualifications.* [online] Available at: https://www.gov.uk/government/publications/english-baccalau-reate-eligible-qualifications [Accessed 29 Jan. 2024].

10
Big A Little A

Why Core Skills Matter

Crass

If you like a bit of anarchy, then Crass is for you. Crass is also for you if you want the punk lyrical artistry of George Orwell; they're political, socially aware, beautiful and angry.

'Big A Little A' encourages a resistance to those that would control you – politicians, religion, figures of authority (teachers?). Be yourself, not a prisoner to the system and those who are out to 'get you'.

Crass drummer Penny Rimbaud explains, 'Punk ain't a fashion, it's a way of being, it's anarchy in the UK, the USA, wherever, and that isn't tuned guitars and voices in harmony any more than it's limousines at stage doors.'

Saying that of course, I'm also an English teacher and a bit of a pedant. So, yeah, anarchy and chaos are great but use the correct grammar and punctuation please. For me, you need to get your big A and little a sorted because it matters: language is the battlefield of the revolution. And if you don't think so, consider how weaponised the word *woke* has become. For punk leaders, SPⒶG matters.

Of course, core skills do not *personally* matter for everyone despite what they might publicly advocate for. In the past year I have reviewed many applications for senior leadership posts, including one from a 'Vice Principle', one addressing me as 'Mr Featherston' and countless others who don't seem aware that their names and addresses should contain capital letters. In these cases I really struggle to turn the page. If student literacy, oracy, numeracy and digital competency are important, then you have to live these values. If you're about to go for a job where you advocate for core skills but can't actually be bothered yourself then I'm going to find it hard to believe you; that really is crass and not in a good way.

For our young people, a secure grasp of these essential skills demonstrates to future employers that they can communicate with precision; it's not all about employers but I also appreciate that not everyone becomes impassioned about the Oxford comma. We do not want any of our children to be 'a prisoner in the boundaries they set you' and therefore an education that values core skills *alongside* knowledge is a fundamental right for all.

Literacy

Even as an experienced English teacher, I bloody hate teaching literacy. Spelling, punctuation and grammar is boring. I don't know how to ever make apostrophes exciting, and this is not a book about Punk Literacy. Certainly, I have found slightly less tedious ways over the years to teach the rules and conditions, and how to apply them, but nothing revolutionary. The English language is in a continual state of evolution, influenced by hundreds of other languages over the years, and therefore accuracy is not always a given.

Too many people are not confident readers. An Ofsted review of reading education in England's prisons in 2022[1] suggested that up to 50% of the population could not read well enough to access a Level 1 course. Not everyone who cannot read competently ends up in prison but not having this skill closes down far too many routes in life.

We have to get this right with our very youngest learners in school. Not every child arrives loving books and reading but quite quickly those that *can* start to move away from those that *cannot*. The work of professionals in EYFS (Early Years Foundation Stage) is the most important in the world of education but is too often dismissed. I'm not an expert but am in awe of those that work with these children; we need to stop trying to get four-year-olds learning facts at desks. They need to play, experiment, explore, learn to love learning itself. When children become suspicious of reading, when it becomes another thing they're not getting right and have difficulty with, they do everything they can to avoid it; they resent it and stop engaging. When this happens to a young child, their reading growth stops. So why do we have an education system that often forces kids into hating reading and writing? If oracy matters, why is speaking and listening no longer properly assessed in GCSE English?

Obviously, there are a plethora of learning needs that can affect a child's (or an adult's) ability to read confidently. Punk leaders know that every child is an individual, and every individual should have their needs met, not glossed over. We have a statutory responsibility to adapt learning for children with special education needs but more than that, it is an ethical duty; no one left behind, especially not because it is a bit of a chore.

Numeracy

At least with literacy I'm an English specialist; with numeracy it is a foreign field. I don't know when it went wrong for me and maths; perhaps because English was always my strongest subject maths automatically became my worst? In the primary school classroom, I didn't dislike maths, but I worked through it slowly and disliked being rushed; therefore, I never fully grasped what everyone else understood and the next lesson would pick up two paces ahead of where I'd left off.

Mostly, I quite enjoy numbers. There is a lot of maths in my job: finance, student numbers, attendance, salaries, outcomes, what percentage of students who have special educational needs are also eligible for free school meals ... I love a good graph or pie chart and I cannot imagine many jobs in the world where a rudimentary understanding of numeracy is not required, although knowing how to use a calculator is often enough.

I lost my way with maths when stuff like trigonometry and algebra started turning up. I could do some of it but, again, I never got far enough and then the lesson would resume further ahead than my understanding. Did I ever truly need to understand these things – probably not although my maths teacher friends will vociferously argue with me on that. I suppose they never truly needed to understand pathetic fallacy in *Wuthering Heights* either.

Without a doubt literacy and numeracy skills are critical – but do we diverge too much from what is truly needed in order to expand laterally into subject specialist content we probably don't need to survive? A wholesale overview of the English qualifications system is needed but who is brave enough to chuck out Shakespeare and quadratic equations? If you love it, if you choose it, learn deeper – but is it essential for everyone at a time when there is so much more needed in the modern curriculum? When we only have so much time, let's prioritise *everyone* being confident in literacy and numeracy rather than a few being brilliant, leaving the rest behind.

Digitally Speaking

If ever there was a more chaotic and misunderstood core skill it is digital literacy. Depending on who you are speaking to they might prioritise online safety and responsible social media use, or being able to recognise and respond to fake news, or being able to code like an app designer or simply being able to attach a CV to a job application email.

Of course, it is all of this, and more. However, we barely have enough time for trigonometry let alone properly embedding these skills in the day-to-day curriculum. Time is the least of our problems currently; very few schools have sufficient technology to make it available for everyone needing it. Yes, in many homes there is fast broadband and a PC, a laptop, maybe a tablet and everyone has a smart phone but there are huge numbers of homes where this is not the case. For many families there may be a phone each, but they are possibly running off shared data.

This made trying to teach online during the global pandemic almost impossible. In England, eventually a few laptops came through, but no one was fitting broadband in their homes either. In April 2020 we calculated we needed nearly 700 laptops plus almost as many dongles to provide equal access to online learning for all the children in our school; by the summer we had four. Eighteen months later we had around half the number needed, and these came in dribs and drabs. Many children endured lockdown with no access to regular online learning because even if they were one of the lucky ones, the laptops were issued to families and children had to share.

Although the same can be said for cross-curricular literacy, without a doubt adult confidence and competence when it comes to digital literacy is another huge barrier within schools. At the turn of the century, I remember hearing that, 'In twenty years there will be two types of teacher: the digitally literate and the retired', but that has not quite come to pass. As a profession we are far more skilled than we used to be, but probably not as much as the children we teach. Certainly, old, tired technology is what most schools have to endure and it too frequently goes wrong. When tech goes wrong, your average teacher is not skilled enough to put it right and eventually they will avoid it completely for fear of having the lesson completely wrecked.

If our young people learning good, strong, safe digital skills is a priority for them to participate in the modern world (and, hey, this is the twenty-first century after all), then investment is essential – and this stuff is not cheap. Investment is needed in the technology itself, in training, in ensuring access is equitable and not based on parental affluence. Then the curriculum itself has to be both realistic and appropriate: what needs to be taught to our young people for them to participate in the world, adapted as the world changes, and leaving no one behind.

Punk leadership suggests

- A confident grasp of core skills is the gateway to a wide-open world of opportunities for young people; it is criminal to allow anything to get in the way of that. Without these core skills we are boxing children within stifling boundaries.

- Resource each core skill properly: finance it, allocate curriculum time, train staff properly, ensure everyone can access it, don't let children move on until they've got it.

- When needs be, slow learning down so that core skills can be fully grasped, but also enjoyed; we do not need to rush through content at the risk of leaving people behind and insecure.

- If it matters – show it and use it yourself.

Note

1   Ministry of Justice. (2022) *Prison Education: A Review of Reading Education in Prisons*. [online] Available at: https://www.gov.uk/government/publications/prison-education-a-review-of-reading-education-in-prisons/prison-education-a-review-of-reading-education-in-prisons [accessed 29 Jan. 2024].

11
Sex & Drugs & Rock & Roll

Whole Child Education

The Inclusive Curriculum

Punk is often criticized for being a bunch of angry white boys. Although that is largely true, there are plenty of punks of all races, colours, genders, sexualities, abilities and languages. It is a fully inclusive subculture; without a doubt it is not without a few knobs, but there is also something for everyone and no entry requirements to the community. If you want to be a punk, you can be one.

Ian Dury contracted polio aged seven which resulted in the paralysis and withering of his left leg, shoulder and arm. He attended a grammar school, his mother eschewing Chailey, a school and hospital for disabled children that mainly taught trades. His experience there was far from idyllic, often being subjected to horrendous punishments; at 16 he went to Walthamstow College of Art and found his way into lecturing, professional art and music.

'Sex & Drugs & Rock & Roll' was released in 1977 and immediately banned by the BBC whilst simultaneously being championed by several of its DJs including Annie Nightingale and John Peel. Often misunderstood, it is not a hedonistic anthem celebrating only a life of excess, but rather a reminder not to be a slave to the 9–5 job and those that will 'trap you with the ordinary'.

More than ever children need an expansive, open, inclusive, diverse and honest curriculum. Dury's lyrical advice includes 'don't do nothing that is cut price'. This doesn't refer to money; rather, not cutting corners, taking the easy way out, doing anything by halves. What Hywel Roberts, citing American academic Martin Haberman, would call 'the pedagogy of poverty'. This is children's one go at education and we have a responsibility to make it special, exciting, relevant and engaging; the curriculum we create will set them up for the rest of their lives, fostering curiosity and a love of learning forever. And yes, that should include sex and drugs and rock and roll.

Rock and Roll

The arts have been slowly vanished from the curriculum. Not everywhere of course; there are schools whose Phonics Check, or Key Stage 2 Scaled Scores, or EBacc measures won't be too adversely affected if they continue giving over whole afternoons to the recorder or ceramics. But when progress measures carry such risk to schools, who can blame them for chopping what is not examined?

I once visited a very highly performing primary school and their success, according to the proud headteacher, was that every morning every child had Reading, Writing and Maths. Teachers marked over their lunch time and children that didn't *get it* were re-taught in the afternoon whilst their peers consolidated their learning through cross-curricular topics such as Volcanos and Science-in-a-Tray.

Yes, kids have to be able to read, write, calculate, speak confidently, but what's the point if there is no art? Why reduce centuries of literature to how well you can analyse an example in 45 minutes; where is the awe and wonder at what musicians and artists can achieve, at what *we* can achieve, unless there is a grade at the end of it?

Many English secondary schools, distressingly alert to Progress-8 and the English Baccalaureate, have reduced the amount of contact time children have outside of English, maths, science, modern foreign languages, geography and history. Furthermore, PE is often completely removed in Key Stage 4 unless students have selected it as an option. Of course, schools have the freedom to choose, but this does not extend to the freedom to choose to ignore league tables and Ofsted. Provisional GCSE and A Level entries for 2023[1] show a shocking decline in take-up of creative subjects in favour of EBacc subjects like computer science. At GCSE, art and design entries are down 3.3%, music fell 11.8%, drama 7.4% and performing arts 16.4%. Interestingly there is an increase for modern languages at GCSE (in the EBacc measures) but this drops off substantially at A level – perhaps schools are narrowing pathways without fostering the love.

The solution for many is that these now marginalised subjects can be a part of the wider, extra curriculum. Children can learn musical instruments, or paint, or play sport, or dance, or cook outside of normal lesson time. This presupposes that there are any staff left not utterly exhausted from their day to run such events, and that children's families have the means to support their extra-curricular choices. Some cannot afford the financial cost of a guitar, a drum kit, music lessons, art supplies, football boots that don't fall apart after a couple of wears or the transport to the next dance competition. And some cannot spare the time: older siblings are required for childcare or other caring duties, some have religious observance, some simply live too far away. Not every child has a room of their own to practise in, or the support to do so. More than once I have consoled a young person because someone in their house has sold equipment that belongs to the school, or smashed it up in a rage.

Again, it is not a level playing field for all our children, which is why all schools must provide access to as many experiences as possible for them. If we don't do it, no one will.

Jolly Bad Show

Likewise, getting *out* of school is a wonderful and exclusive experience, so long as children can afford it. I remember being 16 and learning about two wonderful trips that the school was running: one to the Austrian Alps to ski and one to Egypt. I didn't even bring the letters home for my parents as there would have been no way we could ever have afforded either. Heartbreakingly, I know they might have tried to afford the Egypt one as I have long had a fascination with ancient history; this would have just made me feel guilty and embarrassed. How many trips does your school run that are genuinely affordable to all children? It's not punk to price kids out of an experience, especially if no one else is going to provide it for them.

When my husband worked in business, his company arranged a day trip for the workers after a particularly good year. Standing on the beach front, one of the 40-year-old packers surveyed the sand and sea. 'Must have taken ages to put all this in', he marvelled, having never been to the seaside before and not understanding that the beach was a natural phenomenon. Since then, we have taken the whole of Year 7 to the seaside for free every year, no one pays. Usually it is wonderful and life affirming, even if I'm on a four-hour toilet duty. Once, after having a chip stolen by a seagull, one child did tell me it was 'the worst day of his life ever'.

You won't believe the experiences some children never have. We arranged another free trip in December, taking students into Birmingham by train to visit the Central Library and the Christmas Markets. We knew some would never have been on a train, or into the city just five miles from where they lived, but three of them had never been on an escalator and were so terrified they grabbed hold of strangers.

Punk leaders identify and prioritise these out-of-the-classroom experiences for all children, making them as accessible as possible. We accompany these trips as well; it makes a huge difference to other staff and the children themselves for us to sit on a coach for hours, or camp next to them on a residential, or fall over in a stream during a geography field trip. I've pretty much organised, initiated, or accompanied every type of trip there is and I cannot recommend them enough. But not skiing; I'm not stupid.

In her 2018 blog, Christine Counsell explored the ideas of Core and Hinterland knowledge; these are not binary opposites but interwoven, each making the other stronger. Core knowledge comprises those facts that need to be learnt and retained, and often assessed. The Hinterland provides context, a deeper meaning, a real-world example or a hook to help make the core knowledge relatable.

- Gravity is the force that attracts a body towards the centre of the earth: core knowledge. Hinterland knowledge might include the anecdote about Isaac Newton's apple, or who fell over in the playground.

- World War II took place between 1939 and 1945: core knowledge. Talking to older relatives about their experiences during the Blitz and of Evacuation, or being privileged to have a Holocaust survivor visit the class is the Hinterland.

The Hinterland curriculum must be woven into children's school experiences because not all have equal access outside of school. For some, their understanding of core knowledge has no context, no frame in which it can be seen as important or memorable. Luckily humans love stories, more so children, and so deliberate planning to weave Hinterland and Core is an essential teacher act; time for this has to be provided by us punk leaders and not left to chance.

Sex and Drugs

Willies and boobs and bums and condoms and consent and gender identity and puberty and coke and weed and tobacco and vapes... Should we even be teaching this stuff in schools? I mean, isn't this the domain of parents and carers? In an ideal world, yes, but this is far from an ideal world. In some homes girls still have their first period and think they're dying, teenagers still use dubious birth control, some would still rather kill themselves than come out as gay or transgender. And weed is legal right?

Many teachers *hate* teaching what I'll broadly call PSHE – personal, social, health education. They do *not* want to have to teach giggling teenagers about birth control, especially if they ask personal questions; this is a time when teachers absolutely do not wish to combine Core and Hinterland knowledge. I remember a Deputy Headteacher teaching me this when I was about 13: 'You can ask me anything you like', he said, 'Except for personal things like how often my wife and I have sex', which absolutely guaranteed no one in that room asked *any questions at all* and it also put me off my muffin that I was sneaking under the table.

However, punk leaders do not shy away from difficult and controversial topics; we ask the adults in our schools to step up for the children who do not live in open or supportive homes because, quite literally, it will save lives.

Staff need training, lots of training, and really clear shared plans. I wouldn't advocate throwing an inexperienced teacher into a room of 12-year olds and leave them to it for an hour on the topic of consent. And consent is not something you can teach once and tick off. At its best PSHE is done sensitively but factually. Don't dumb anything down because some of these children have knowledge and experiences well beyond their years. Don't assume the adults know everything they have to teach; sadly, some do not know the difference between vagina, vulva, clitoris, cervix, urethra and anus.

Agree the terminology you will use for your school, share with all stakeholders and do not veer from what you know to be right. School leaders remember with horror the extended abuse experienced by staff at Anderton Park Primary School in Birmingham when their gentle and age-appropriate LGBTQIA+ curriculum was misinterpreted by outsiders determined to cause trouble. Headteacher Sarah Hewitt-Clarkson and her team are proper punk leaders: they knew what they were doing was absolutely the right thing and would not be bullied, it would have been all too easy to simply capitulate but that would not have been in the best interests of the children.

So, no, we probably shouldn't be teaching this shit but we *have to* because children need access to sensitive, inclusive, honest and accurate education in a safe space with safe non-judgemental adults.

Punk leadership suggests

- That all schools should maintain a wide and inclusive curriculum despite accountability measures that make it far easier to ditch anything not *essential*.
- Personal, social, health, emotional, sexual, identity education is critical. Punk leaders do what is right for all children; an inclusive and open approach saves lives.
- Not all children can attend after-school clubs and activities and punk leaders find solutions to enable them to participate.
- Find a way to get all kids out of school.

Note

1 Department for Education (2023) *Provisional Entries for GCSE, AS and A level: Summer 2023 Exam Series*. [online] Available at: https://www.gov.uk/government/statistics/provisional-entries-for-gcse-as-and-a-level-summer-2023-exam-series/provisional-entries-for-gcse-as-and-a-level-summer-2023-exam-series [accessed 29 Jan. 2024].

12
Suspect Device
Leading Inclusive Schools

Suss, Suss, Suss

If you grow up in Northern Ireland during The Troubles, do you write songs about your lived experiences or is that exploiting a sectarian conflict that saw hundreds killed?

Stiff Little Fingers wrote their truth despite the backlash. Inspired by other punk bands, singer and songwriter Jake Burns later reflected, 'What The Clash's first album did more than anything else was give me the confidence, through its lyrical subject matter, to realise it was OK to write about my own life and experiences.'[1]

It is bold stuff; for this particular song the pain is that of being judged as a *suspect device* simply for existing in a hostile environment. Sadly, for a lot of children, simply existing in a school can make them feel like a suspect device.

Put up the Wall

An inclusive school does not select its students. It does not select economically – either through slicing off those who can afford to pay fees, for an expensive uniform, for unaffordable compulsory items such as an iPad, or for prohibitive transport to and from school. It does not select based on religion, sex or ability. An inclusive school does not effectively select by compliance; by setting the zero-tolerance bar so high only the most biddable children can survive and thrive.

I suppose the only type of specialist school I can truly understand parents expressing a preference for is a special school to meet a child's complex needs. The utopia would be for all children, even those with complex special needs, to have their needs met through careful adaptions within mainstream schools. Sadly, in the UK at the moment often these children do not have their needs fully met even in small and dedicated specialist schools – but that is about funding and capacity and government policy rather than the will, expertise and commitment of the school itself.

And, of course, parents can choose to send their children to school wherever they wish. Over the course of my own educational journey I have attended rough-as-you-like comprehensives, a tiny village school where I was one of only two girls in my year and the private independent Munich International School when my dad got a job abroad for a bit. I've also worked in a range of schools, from an all-through 3–16 provision in a deprived white working-class estate, to leafy Warwickshire and Worcestershire suburbs to huge multi-cultural secondaries.

I've loved most of the schools I either attended as a student or worked in. Without a doubt the most enjoyable schools I have spent time in are the truly inclusive, those that don't put up walls to keep suspect devices out. In any given day you may encounter all sexes, genders, religions and ethnicities; you might teach a small group of truly gifted A Level students who will stretch your own intellect; a class of students who might struggle to even read.

Inflammable Material

Too often schools are looking only for children who are non-flammable material; those that won't provide a challenge in terms of behaviour, attendance or outcomes. To be inflammable material is too much of a risk. These schools can look attractive to parents too, those that don't want their children mixing with the wrong sort for fear of contagion. Too often we judge schools by the demographic they serve or by success measures stacked against us.

This is not to say any punk leader advocates for lower standards, slower progress and lesser outcomes for any child; indeed often we want something far more ambitious. However, the reality is that there is an advantage gap between children right from birth – prenatal care, access to experienced midwives, regular health checks, early years provision. A child growing up in a home where health workers were barred from entering and with no books to look at will have further to climb upon reaching school than a child regularly read to, conversed with and fed healthily. The economic status of a child's home does not determine their intelligence or potential, but it can certainly place them at different starting points where academic outcomes are concerned.

In many ways I am alluding to children eligible for free school meals (although that bar is far too low given how many children live in poverty) and also those that the school receives additional Pupil Premium funding for (i.e. those that have ever received free school meals at any point over the last six years of school). The adage goes that the more Pupil Premium children a school has, the lower the results and the more challenging the behaviour of children and their families. Although this can be broadly true, the vast majority of so-called Pupil Premium children and their families are bloody lovely and that well-heeled lawyer parent can really kick off via email after a few glasses of *Whispering Angel* on a Friday evening.

As an experienced leader who has worked in all kinds of schools, I can absolutely confirm that many of your professional peers will judge you, your school and your ability to lead effectively based on the demographic of the school you work in. I remember vividly introducing myself to senior leaders in a new local authority and seeing their faces drop when I told them my school's name; they pitied me and some either never gave me the time of day or repeatedly patronised me. It was as if leaders were divided into tiers with the very best going to wholly middle-class schools and the rubbish ones left to work in schools with more children on free school meals than not. Wankers.

Without a doubt, some schools are more challenging to work in than others but that is no reason not to give it a go. I have found them far more rewarding, as if what I do really will have a lasting impact on the lives of children even if they don't appear terribly grateful at the time; I certainly don't expect to be the educated white saviour sweeping in to conduct charity work with poor families who know no better. Don't alter your values and vision for success when working in more challenging or inclusive schools but do review the timescale, the path, and be kind to yourself and others.

Why Can't They all Just Clear Off

Alarmingly, some schools will advertise themselves as inclusive but in reality this is a thin PR veneer. They will tell parents that they welcome children with special educational needs but upon further exploration this will actually mean compliant children whose special educational needs cause no behaviour problems. Usually, this means children with social, emotional and mental health needs (SEMH), speech, language and communication needs (SLCN) and some children on the Autistic spectrum.

I've heard it said at Open Evenings: *we're not great with children with SEMH or SLCN or ASD but School X down the road is brilliant with them*. So loving parents will go to School X down the road and ask if they can meet the needs of their child – and if they are truly inclusive the answer will be: *yes, we'll try*. And the first school will have some special educational needs children, and claim they are inclusive, and feature children with hearing aids or that use wheelchairs on their publicity … but they aren't inclusive at all.

The high-stakes combination of published outcomes and Ofsted judgements mean that we are in a vicious circle of some schools wanting the *high-quality* creamed-off students and their families only – which then makes them more appealing to parents looking to be part of the cream. We have some students travelling miles to get to a *better* school when actually most schools do a great job and it is parents that can have the biggest influence over a child's success at school.

No child, no family, no school should be viewed as a *suspect device* to be avoided or damaging to the reputation of a school. Punk leaders actively work to make this happen through leading truly inclusive schools.

To achieve inclusion you have to work with other leaders also committed to inclusion – therefore choose your school, your local authority, your multi-academy trust very carefully. This is a battle you cannot win alone as often the battle is too great: think 'Battle of the Bastards' in *Game of Thrones*.

Inclusive rhetoric has to be shared and articulated by everyone in the institution rather than just a few. This means teachers have to know that a child's disruptive behaviour has a reason and although their behaviour may not be tolerated and allowed to disrupt others' learning, the child can't just be made to vanish and never seen again. You cannot *throw away* children – there is nowhere for them to go. By working with them you can include them back into lessons and they can be successful.

Building positive relationships with children and their parents takes time. Often when talking to colleagues that have just started at my school, and may be finding it tough, I tell them: *be patient, stick at it, be consistent, see what it's like returning after the holiday*. And after Christmas the children recognise their face, know they haven't abandoned them and have committed; consequently, things are easier. More so after Easter. And come the new school year it can be like a different school.

Just last week I was speaking to a fairly experienced teacher who joined us in September. She took over a Year 10 class and, in her words, they were *vile*. At best she would get a couple of written sentences out of them per lesson. But she persevered and they have just completed their end of year exams. Every student wrote pages and pages in response to the questions and came out beaming, wanting to tell her about how well they had done. The tears of frustration and anger in September are now tears of pride and joy; it's cheesy but it's true and completely rewarding.

Punk leaders make this happen. We talk to staff, we talk to students, we resolve conflict and offer support but we don't deviate from the commitment to inclusion. We encourage and provide frameworks for children and teachers to succeed. It is utterly exhausting but it's some of the most important work there is.

Punk leaders also know that usually, behind every challenging child there can be a challenging parent, and often one in need. We talk about *hard to reach parents* but actually are we a hard to reach school? We cannot be truly inclusive if we don't include parents, carers and the wider family. We have to make parents feel welcome coming into school; the only time we call them cannot be when their child has misbehaved or caused an issue. We need to acknowledge that for some parents their own schooling was traumatic and just coming to the gates is a big deal – why don't we go out to them instead?

And of course, to be truly inclusive, it has to be resourced and funded appropriately, which a whole different battle.

Punk leadership suggests

- Schools should not be selective by ability, gender, religion, economics or special need, but to achieve this all schools need adequate funding and resourcing to support all children properly.
- Punk leaders persist stubbornly in their inclusivity despite pressures around them not to be.
- For those schools pretending to be inclusive, call them out on it.
- Punk leaders in inclusive schools will be judged by their peers for the schools they work in and the children that attend them but don't be deterred, what you're doing is often exhausting but also truly exhilarating.

Note

1   Link, R. (2009) *Kicking Up a Racket: The Story of Stiff Little Fingers 1977–83.* Belfast: Appletree Press, p. 41.

13
If the Kids Are United

Leading Schools Where Children Have a Voice

Sham

Sham 69 were a pretty successful seventies punk band, scoring five top twenty hits in the UK charts and even getting on *Top of the Pops*. They've disbanded, reformed and changed line-ups so often it feels like most maths departments. Co-founder and front man Jimmy Pursey remained a stable fixture of a band, rooted in the streets and football terraces. These can be heard on 'If the Kids Are United' and lend the song, and this chapter, some authenticity.

The band stopped performing live after a shambolic gig at the Rainbow Theatre in Finsbury Park when the stage was rushed by white power skinheads. Sham 69's music had been born from punk but attracted a skinhead following – right-wing, left-wing and no-wing; they were later influenced by more mainstream British rock. Certainly I have spent many an enjoyable three minutes or so jumping around to this song (If the Kids are United by Sham 69), probably causing my knees an awful lot of damage.

Interestingly, when talking about his 1980 album *The Game*, Pursey pretty much sums up what it is like to work on something without moral purpose, which applies to any profession including teaching:

> I was forced into making it, you understand? I called it *The Game* because that's how the music business had become to me. Like a little roulette wheel where everything we did had all of this political value to it, but it didn't make any difference because you spin the wheel and if it landed on the right number you were all right, the wrong number and you were not all right.[1]

And that's why we need punk leaders, not bland homogenous ones.

I've Got Something to Say

When we consider student voice, we don't solely mean children talking. Some children talk a great deal, indeed you can hardly shut them up, whereas others barely open their mouths. Talking a lot, and actually having something meaningful to say about their lives are two different things.

It is also not simply the tick-box Student Council. Our student council has one representative from every tutor group but that's only around 3% of the school population. With two from each tutor group that's still only 6% and that's hardly representative. After all, student voice is not Parliament.

Add to that *who* is actually chosen to join the student council, and why: is it the loudest? Is it the most passionate? The most articulate? The one with most friends? The one the tutor would quite like out of their classroom every now and again?

As Simon Sinek would encourage, start with your *why*; why do you want students to have a voice in your school? What will giving them a voice achieve? Will it achieve anything other than being listened to or could it effect genuine change? How will students know they have made a change? How do you ensure *all* voices are included rather than just those that shout loudest?

I think student voice matters immensely; as school is something young people experience, they should have some agency over aspects of it. School, education, should not be something they passively endure with no say over it. Sure, they cannot control everything – school leaders have things that are out of their control – but there needs to be an agreement as to what things they can influence.

Here are a few things we have tried over the years, some more successfully than others; they are offered as starting points and great punk leaders will steal off the shelf, adapt for their setting or ignore completely – and that's fine.

Up and Down and Across

Our students are organised into year groups, Years 7 to 11 and the Sixth Form. In addition, they are also in Houses, with two tutor groups per year belonging to each House (except the Sixth Form, which has one tutor group per House). This is still not a wide and inclusive democracy. Does this mean that the student council in your school is year-based? Or vertically House-based? Why not *both?* True democracy aims to include everyone.

With clear purposes and agendas, each council can discuss different aspects of the school. In a school as big as ours getting the whole council of 55 students together would be an immense mission but smaller schools can do this far more easily.

Regardless, what matters is that they *do* meet; nothing demoralises student voice more than the keenness to contribute and the means to do so never actually being offered. Calendar the meetings at the start of the year, just like staff meetings, and then make sure they happen.

The Disenfranchised

Alongside any regular student council, consider who the disenfranchised children are who need a voice more than anything; a safe space to be who they are, feel supported and work on aspects of their experience at school that will make it better for future generations. And then open these self-selecting groups up to anyone who wants to come along.

At my current school we call these student advocate groups and each is run by a member of staff who is a great role model and passionate about ensuring these young people are heard. This year we have run the following student advocate groups: LGBTQIA+, Anti-Bullying Champions, Anti-Racism and Anti-Sexism. Next year students have additionally asked for a Positive Mental Health group, one for children with SEND and an Inter-Faith group who want to organise a Culture Day.

Our LGBTQIA+ group is particularly active, but this does not mean there is no homophobia in the school. Sadly, it is likely to be a long time before that particular discrimination is not embedded in all aspects of society. However, the students have organised our Pride Month for the last three years, making each successive one larger and involving more people than before. They run assemblies with other students and training with staff. They invited the new Mayor in on Rainbow Day to be part of the celebrations.

Money, Money, Money

As we all know, to really make a difference in schools you often need money. Student councils are very good at identifying how money could be spent but are often in the position where they have to ask the grown-ups to make the purchase – and this means that the grown-ups can veto it.

So how can we ensure that students have some money of their own to effect some of the changes they want to see?

One year when we had slightly underspent on a particular budget, I awarded each year group £1000 to spend on items they themselves identified as being needed. If nothing else, they learnt that £1000 doesn't go far in education.

They invested in picnic tables, new books in the library, extra PE equipment and, for the Sixth Form, a water cooler and coffee machine.

It is not often that we underspend at school – so it is also possible, *so long as very clearly communicated with all stakeholders in advance*, that on charity days half of the money raised can go to the named charity and half to the student council. Often, children will work doubly hard to fundraise, knowing that they are investing in themselves as well as worthy charities.

Involving older students in applying for small grants is also a great thing to do; what an amazing experience to add to college, university, job or apprenticeship applications. Using curriculum time to do this is reasonable – through PSHE, Citizenship or similar – with students developing real skills bringing in real money for student-identified projects.

Get professional

Everyone from the British Council to the NASUWT to the House of Lords all value student voice and leadership, providing frameworks and resources to make your school's provision more professional if that's your goal. The Lords in Schools[2] initiative is a great platform to encourage discussions about democracy and how Parliament works.

You can also spend a small fortune on arranging specialist leadership training for your young people; I participated in this many years ago and it provided a very clear structure: the various leadership roles and their purpose; writing an agenda; evaluating impact. It's useful if setting up from scratch or you have a strong team; undoubtedly you need an organised member of staff that will quietly maintain it behind the scenes.

Online canvassing

One way to encourage *all* students to have a voice is to seek out their views online; yes, they may need their school email addresses to log in but beyond that it is anonymous, thus ensuring students can be completely honest.

You have to ensure that all students can access the online platform you are using, so something accessible on a phone with minimal data is ideal. Not all students have access to Wi-Fi, a laptop or PC or even their own device.

The questions have to be clear, accessible to all abilities and worded so that you are learning about their views regarding something specific. Too many questions, or those with lots of free-text boxes can be off putting to students and unhelpful to you.

What do you think of school? A free text box will garner everything from, 'It's shit', to an essay on why Ms Hussain's science lessons are the best in the world.

Do you like school? Yes, No. Maybe. (Maybe? What the heck is that?). I think I could tell you the answers now to be honest.

On an average day, how safe do you feel in school, with 1 being really safe all the time and 5 being never safe? That is starting to get some more useful data and, if cross-referenced with year group and protected characteristics, you can start to build a better picture of the school.

For anything more detailed, *talk* to them.

The Panel

This really freaks some teachers out: including a student panel as part of the interview process. No, the children are not *interviewing* candidates, they are asking them questions. No, the children are not choosing which person gets the job, *you* are seeing how they interact with a range of young people not in a classroom setting. And kids ask some cracking questions.

You are also providing students with the opportunity to experience what a job interview is *really* like and so long as you don't use the same *nice* kids every time then you widen that opportunity whilst giving interviewees a chance to chat to your young people.

Children obviously don't make the final decision but to give them a voice is terrifically powerful; they feel that they have influenced who works with them and this only has a positive impact when they meet again in the classroom, or on the late gate. It helps to build positive respectful relationships.

Freedom is Given

But really, why are we the adults even deciding what student voice should look like in a school? If we truly advocated for student voice, we would be asking the children themselves what they would prefer. They may not have any models to hand, but with a few examples they will express a preference. With the support of senior leaders and dedicated champions they will make a fantastic success of it. Give children the freedom to articulate their voice and you will reap the rewards.

Punk leadership suggests

- That all children must be given a voice in their school on the things that matter to them; find a way to ensure that student voice is truly representative of your entire community and not just a small demographic.
- Find ways to enable young people to be the punk leaders of the future: being prefects, being classroom monitors, being sports or academic or artistic champions, being involved in interviews or sitting on councils.
- Ensure students can actually make a difference themselves; find a way to provide them with any resource they choose for themselves and don't veto it (unless it is truly bonkers).
- Punk leaders know that the school in which we work is never *our* school; it only ever belongs to the children that attend it and we have to trust in their drive and ambition to make it the best it can be.

Notes

1 Kowalewski, A.I. (1989) *Jimmy Pursey 1988: Sham 69 Round Two: A Decade to Think*, Flipside, whole no. 58 (Winter 1989), pp. 24–27.
2 UK Parliament. (n.d.) *Learn with the Lords in School.* [online] Available at: https://learning.parliament.uk/en/session-workshop/learn-with-the-lords-in-school/ [Accessed 29 Jan. 2024].

14
I Fought the Law
Managing Student Behaviour

Operation Just Cause

Legend has it that in 1989, during the U.S. military's mission to force Manuel Noriega from power in Panama, they blasted The Clash's version of 'I Fought the Law' at his stronghold.

Written in 1958 by Sonny Curtis, the song was originally recorded by The Crickets and later by the Bobby Fuller Four in 1965. Possibly the most popularly known version by The Clash was released as part of their *Cost of Living* EP in 1979. Around the same time, The Dead Kennedys released a version with changed lyrics which includes, *I am the law, so I won*, prompted when Harvey Milk and George Moscone were murdered by San Francisco politician Dan White. The Dead Kennedys saw White as a man with authority who got away with pre-meditated murder because of a successful diminished responsibility defence. There are other versions too; listen to them all, they're fab.

Humbled

> [Young people] are high-minded because they have not yet been humbled
> by life, nor have they experienced the force of circumstances ... They
> think they know everything, and are always quite sure about it. (*Rhetoric
> Part 12 On Youthful Character*, Aristotle, 4th Century BC).[1]

We have been grumbling about youth for centuries; each generation believing that they were far more respectful, polite, studious and hard-working than the youth following. I don't know about you, but I *know* I was a pain in the arse as a kid and my own daughter is a huge improvement to the gene pool.

Perhaps there is something in Aristotle's assertion that we become humbled by life as we get older but one of education's enduring battlegrounds is whether schools themselves should deliberately humble children as part of their education.

Children's behaviour is consistently the number one concern for adults working in schools; this is regardless of location or the type of school you may work at. Also, anecdotally, staff believe that behaviour is getting worse with each successive year. 'In 2022, 1 in 5 teachers (20%) said student behaviour was the biggest source of stress, this has now risen to 1 in 4 (25%).'[2]

Given that it is consistently one of teachers' biggest stressors, it is unsurprising that schools devote such time and energy to finding solutions to poor behaviour. After all, it can be seen that better behaviour = less stressed teachers = better recruitment and retention = less stressed children = better lessons = better behaviour ...

The Battleground

A boy must hold his tongue among his elders. (*Clouds* by Aristophanes, 423BC)[3]

In the realm of education, social media, another false dichotomy, has weighed in around the issues of how best to tackle poor student behaviour and even what behaviours are undesirable in the first place. Some argue that teachers have a duty to enforce strict rules, deliberately humble children and 'flatten the grass'[4] in order to make them comply with no-tolerance expectations: silent corridors, looking at teachers in the eye if asked to, no slouching, harsh sanctions for even small demeanours. Without a doubt, penalties and screaming in some children's faces may bring order to what was once a literal battlefield and many welcome it.

Conversely, others argue that the only way to improve student behaviour in the long term is to develop strong respectful relationships and a sense of safety and belonging for all children; it means providing support if a child is struggling to regulate, lending a pen to those without rather than setting a detention and accepting that school corridors will be noisy places even if orderly.

Every person reading this with have their own view on what works best and I suspect most will instinctively be drawn to the middle ground: strong boundaries, clear rules, good routines for learning, consequences for those that are wilfully defiant, alongside warm, respectful relationships, flexibility and being a little bendy with the rules given different children's needs, families and contexts. That's not the soft bigotry of low expectations for the most vulnerable; it is compassion.

What Matters?

> Our sires' age was worse than our grandsires'. We, their sons, are more
> worthless than they; so in our turn we shall give the world a progeny yet
> more corrupt. (Book III of *Odes*, Horace, circa 20 BC)[5]

Without a doubt student behaviour matters. Supporting children to get their behaviour right matters, partly because an unruly adult tends to get into scrapes in the real world as well as poor behaviour making a school feel unsafe for other children and adults. And because it matters, punk leaders should take it seriously and not be happy with a playground or classroom more akin to a mosh-pit. Our duty is to make things better for others, including the misbehaving children themselves.

Working with the full staff team, but also parents and carers as well as the children themselves, come to a consensus about what your school's clear routines, expectations, boundaries, behaviours and responsibilities are. It's not a democracy of course, *you* lead the school and make the final decision, but consultation is an inclusive and important practice to aid with a sense of belonging and ownership.

Whatever rules and expectations you finalise, these have to be fair, clearly and regularly articulated and fairly applied to all. Fair does not always mean identical; I believe in some flexibility depending on a child's circumstances. Equity not equality. After all, wouldn't we as employees expect some understanding if we were late to work after a partner walked out on our relationship, or were a little snappy after a bereavement?

So, I won't tell you what rules and expectations you should have, you and your school are more than capable of determining that; just don't be a dick about it.

Uniformly

> Modern fashions seem to keep on growing more and more debased.
> (*Essays in Idleness*, Yoshida Kenkō, 1330–1332)[6]

Writing this from the United Kingdom, we have very odd expectations around school uniform. I don't have any problems with the concept of uniform in general, after all it helps with a sense of identity and belonging just as a sports team or public service would have.

Like any other agreed expectation, it matters. If you are going to have a uniform it should be adhered to and all should know what the consequences are for not being dressed for school, with, again, a little bit of bendiness. More than once a child has arrived at school not wearing uniform because something traumatic has prevented it: a house fire, being taken into emergency care, even a drug-addicted parent selling it to fuel their habits – kindness matters.

For those unable to afford replacement items, simply have a stock of loan items, of donated vintage items that can be given, or just buy some from the school budget. Currently, we buy every new Year 7 child a full uniform except shoes and for those receiving free school meals they also get a PE kit. Should parents experience financial difficulties during the course of their time here, we have vouchers available for the uniform shop and a local shoe shop; we don't expect anyone to fill in a hardship fund application – that is demeaning, and it deliberately slows the process down. We know our families and we know when they need support.

Largely stereotyping, independent schools in the UK mostly have very formalised uniforms – think Eton. Under the guise of aspiration and ambition, schools in more deprived areas, particularly those that may have been in challenging circumstances, often tend to try and copy the independent school aesthetic: striped or edged blazers with motifs on the breast pocket, tartan skirts, matching bags and coats. Then there are large swathes where everything is a little more relaxed: polo shirts, leggings, sweatshirts, trainers. Again, it doesn't matter so long as it's affordable for all and the rules are applied consistently. If your school says *no trainers* and everyone wears trainers, then what other rules won't be maintained? If you are happy with trainers simply add them to the policy.

We inherit uniform policy from the previous generation of teachers and quite often just maintain it. If it's not a safeguarding or health and safety issue, why legislate it? Piercings and jewellery can cause huge damage to skin. I have seen cut cheeks from rings in fights and a ripped-out lip piercing from it being caught by a passing bag. Artificial nails can really hurt in a fight too, and they can melt in certain science experiments. Shoes need to be sensible for school – resisting rain, dropped equipment in DT or music and solutions in science or art. False eyelashes can't half cause some issues if caught in the face by a dodgeball.

Hair is a typical battlefield and many schools expect everyone to have styles typically worn by white middle-aged people from 1956. Without a doubt, school hair policies disproportionately discriminate against Black children. At one point I simply followed the uniform expectations for hair that had been in place since forever, but I have reflected and if it is not about safeguarding or health and safety then fuck it: dreadlocks, braids, skin-fades, bright red or green, so what? Luckily more and more schools are adopting the Halo Code for hair.[7]

Crime and Punishment

> I am the flail of God. Had you not created great sins, God would not have sent a punishment like me upon you. (Genghis Khan, 1162–1227)[8]

We all remember a teacher with delusions of Genghis Khan. Very rightly we no longer have corporal punishment; both my parents still speak angrily about their own experiences of it, the humiliation and pain, whether it was deserved or not.

We like to punish people in general; as a species we're quite vengeful. We want those that have hurt, wounded or aggrieved us to pay. We maintain the moral high-ground, righteous in our fury, and the anger burns us until we feel they have been equally hurt, wounded or humiliated.

And so it is with children. Many behaviour policies are full of punishments and sanctions without considering whether the consequence for the wrong-doing improves anything. Do detentions really work? I know of some children who fully accept that the consequence for being late to school is a detention that afternoon, but would rather have the lie-in (or drop a young sibling at school) and just finish later. It does not change that they are late every day.

There should be consequences for undesirable behaviours but they should be proportionate and appropriate; they should seek to catch-up missed learning, repair damaged relationships, build an understanding of the positive behaviours we desire to see. Children should be able to learn why repeating their poor behaviour is wrong. If the punishment is designed only to make the child miserable then the resentment – and often the associated behaviours – will simply intensify.

Punk leadership suggests

- Building warm and positive relationships between children and adults should be the foundation of good behaviour in schools.
- All schools need rules and expectations – agree ones that suit your context but then make sure they are clearly explained, that all adults consistently model them and that they are universally fair. Most importantly, do they make sense?
- Consequences matter: be fair, consistent and when needed, a little bendy.
- Find solutions for those that will struggle because of finances rather than simply punishing.
- And remember, 'Children are no longer respectful to their parents', said King Naram Sin of Chaldea in 3800 BC. If they're naughty at school it's probably not just you; work with parents and carers to ensure that your young person grows up to be a responsible, well-adjusted and sensible adult.

Notes

1   The Internet Classics Archive. (n.d.) *Rhetoric* by Aristotle. [online] Available at: http://classics.mit.edu/Aristotle/rhetoric.2.ii.html [Accessed 29 Jan. 2024].

2   Department for Education. (n.d.) *Insight Update: Student Behaviour is Top Stressor for Teachers*. [online] Available at: https://content.govdelivery.com/accounts/UKDFE/bulletins/35eb821 [Accessed 29 Jan. 2024].

3   Aristophanes (c.446–c.386 BC) *Clouds* (Translated by George Theodoridis) [online] Available at: https://www.poetryintranslation.com/PITBR/Greek/Clouds.php [Accessed 28 May 2024].

4   Schoolsweek.co.uk. (2019) *'Flattening the Grass': What's Really Going on?* [online] Available at: https://schoolsweek.co.uk/flattening-the-grass-whats-really-going-on-at-ogat-and-delta/ [Accessed 29 Jan. 2024].

5   Horace (65 BC–8 BC), *The Odes: Book III*. (n.d.) [online] Available at: https://www.poetryintranslation.com/PITBR/Latin/HoraceOdesBkIII.php. [Accessed 29 Jan. 2024].

6   Gillard, J. (2018). The 2,500-Year-Old History of Adults Blaming the Younger Generation [online] Available at: https://historyhustle.com/2500-years-of-people-complaining-about-the-younger-generation/ [Accessed 28 May 2024].

7   Main Page (halocollective.co.uk)

8   Naked History (2016). Genghis Khan in Khwarizm – The Flail of God [online] Available at: https://www.historynaked.com/genghis-khan-khwarizm-flail-god/ [Accessed 28 May 2024].

15
Typical Girls
Gender and Identity in Schools

Feel Like Hell

Punk-reggae all-women band The Slits were gloriously messy in more ways than one. There are a lot more women in punk than the casual observer may imagine, and my own choices for chapter titles suggest.

There is something about the word *slit* that I find deeply uncomfortable; I suspect this is a wide-spread discomfort, which is why the founding musicians selected it as the name for their band: a feminist/punk/rage/cheeky reappropriation of a word that can be used so dismissively and violently to describe female genitals.

'Typical Girls' is a great track and the lyrics still chillingly relatable. Being a typical girl can feel like hell and so can being a typical boy. Thirty years ago, we were trying to smash sexist stereotypes and smash some glass ceilings by warning about images in magazines and encouraging women to take more STEM subjects post-16.

Now … bloody hell it's completely out of control and the paradigm shifts every few hours; it does not take much to get it very wrong indeed. This is not so much a polemic from me screeching about inclusivity (although perhaps it should be) but rather thoughts about how to lead during these challenging times.

Kids First

This chapter is more about gender identity than sexuality or sexism, mainly because there are so many other great books, blogs and podcasts about these matters. Everyone laughs when you talk about *child-centred education*, as if, what else could it be? But you would be surprised; us older people curating an educational experience for our perception of what young people need. We are often wrong, and we have to acknowledge that.

Regardless of any particular views you may have about gender, biological sex, sexuality and identity, these are issues that very much matter to the young people in your school, often at both ends of that spectrum of views.

I cannot fathom why conversations around gender are now dominated by trans concerns, why the greatest trans concerns centre around girls and women, why toilets feature so predominantly, and what the hell furries and rabbit ears have to do with it all.

OK, I can fathom why: partly to blame is right-wing click-bait, some from those that make a career out of being outraged, some emanates from out-dated feminist battle-scars and the rest from people who cannot imagine why people are different to each other, or are happy to be different.

I recently had a lengthy conversation about this issue with a very close friend, a former primary headteacher and feminist. Her central question was: *why are young girls choosing to be boys? Is it a form of internalised misogyny where they have learned it is better to be a boy than a girl?*

My response is simple: I genuinely do not believe *any* child *chooses*; they just *are*. In the same way as sexuality is not chosen, same for gender. It is something innate that some children come to realise sooner than others; some question and later move away from the notion. For some, it's just part of growing up and learning who they are.

Regardless of your own personal beliefs, whether these are religious, political or ideological, leaders in schools have an absolutely fundamental duty to safeguard *every* child in their school. This includes all races, religions, nationalities, abilities, genders and sexual orientations – whether children are certain, questioning or really not sure. It also includes those for whom the 'other' is terrifying or beyond contempt. We are here to be inclusive, support our staff to be inclusive and teach our young people to be inclusive regardless of what a relative, a friend or someone on social media says.

Recently that has been one of the hardest things for leaders to navigate: every child and every family have fiercely entrenched but different views about gender identity in the same way as recently they did about sexuality and further ago about race. It is a conversation not to be shied away from, but one that needs sensitivity and relentless optimism.

I am an inclusive person. I feel very comfortable knowing that children are assigned a sex at birth based on their genitals and that sometimes their biological physiology does not match their gender. Any doctor or biologist will tell you that not all genitals are the same. Differences in sex development, due to genetic and chromosome variations can mean that for some people their genitals develop differently to those of others. Although this is typically not a factor as to whether someone is trans. This discord between the body and the consciousness can result in horrendous confusion, conflict and unhappiness. We know some people are never reconciled and continue to be in crisis with who they are. The impact of this can be tragic.

There is a great deal of evidence to suggest that growing up in a family, school or society that views being trans as a choice and deviation results in worse mental health, alcohol and drug misuse and suicidal thoughts and attempts. If you exist in a world that paints you as a monster and excludes you, of course you're going to be depressed and suicidal. It may also make you angry, an activist, and very vocal. For those who think that suddenly there are lots of trans or non-binary people, perhaps they are simply an emerging voice that has been repressed for far too long.

As it is a safeguarding issue, there are some simple things you can do to support all children.

Who is at Your School?

Do you actually know who is at your school? We will have some information in our management information systems but it's frequently out of date. Quite often as records transfer between schools information is lost or becomes out of date. It is never worth assuming that you know everything about the children in front of you.

We now undertake home-school meetings with all new Year 7 students, all those starting Year 11 or the Sixth Form or that are mid-year transfers. Sometimes these happen at school, sometimes in the family home and sometimes even in a neutral space such as the Asda café. We check all inherited information carefully, then include some questions of our own: particular skills, commitments outside of school, and preferred pronouns. If nothing else, it identifies to all present that we are an inclusive school. We may be with a cis heterosexual female, but she knows too and it doesn't hurt; no one has exploded in shock.

Punks respect pronouns.

Open and ongoing conversations about such things through children's time at school means we can pick up those who start to question and query their identity. Sometimes a cis child will start to query whether they are trans, and over time make some decisions in an environment of care and acceptance; they are not rebelling against anything, or making a panicked decision. Some children join us believing they are gay, and a few years later have reflected that perhaps they are bi-sexual. Kids change, adults change, no one has to have their identity fixed in time: bloody hell, can you imagine what I was like at 12? Or 17? Or 50?

Uniform

This is not a reflection on the concept of uniform, that is elsewhere. However, leaders should ensure that any uniform children are expected to wear is affordable, durable, appropriate and does not insist on forcing children to choose a binary position.

Regardless of what your school's uniform is, any student of any gender should be able to choose any item they feel comfortable in. Trousers, skirts or shorts: every child should choose what they prefer. Ties or cravats: every child should choose what they prefer. Hair: long hair and make-up should not be limited to girls only.

And no, everyone wearing trousers in *not* gender neutral: it is forcing everyone to look the same in a stereotypically male way.

Bog Standards

When I was a relatively young teacher, I accompanied some students on a visit to the House of Lords. I needed the loo. I asked a kindly looking older gentleman where the nearest ladies' was. His response was to look panicked, to explain that they didn't really have many ladies' toilets in the House of Lords, and there was a disabled loo down the corridor I could use. I inferred a great deal about the composition of the Lords from that statement.

Toilets are a very personal and private thing, but they shouldn't be political and they really shouldn't be political in schools. In my home, every toilet is gender neutral; any one can use any toilet. It becomes more complicated for some when the toilets are public and are in gender-specific shared bathrooms, which is what we mostly remember from school: terrifying, smoky (now more vapey), a bully's sanctuary of open space with a few stalls; I certainly avoided them as much as possible.

Leaders do not want children making themselves ill because they are avoiding the use of toilets during the day as entering them makes them feel anxious. This is not limited to having gender-specific toilets. Certainly, having individual toilet stalls, with full-length doors, that anyone can use and that open onto safe spaces is ideal but expensive in terms of cost and space; it also makes them a bully-free zone: no unsighted corners. Only having male and female bathrooms and forcing children to *choose one* is therefore problematic but this is all many schools currently have.

Therefore, consider where some neutral toilets could be placed; we have made most of the toilets previously allocated for disabled users to be inclusive toilets: the door is fully sealed, opens onto the corridor and is for one person at a time. Any student or member of staff may use them regardless of gender or ability.

We've had no problems right from their introduction a couple of years ago and quite a few thanks from parents whose children did not feel comfortable choosing a specific gender. We explained to all students in the school what we were doing and why; some of them may not be terribly pro-trans but perhaps with time it will become more normalised and they will become more inclusive adults.

The Grown-ups

Punk leaders will work with some family members who are vehemently reactionary in terms of gender identity, sexuality and the stereotyping of men, women and different religions and races. For children, we often hear views expressed in the home in lessons and around school, we witness this when they choose Key Stage 4 and 5 options and when they are starting off on their career paths. You can be respectful to the parent themselves without accepting an objectionable opinion because you're not sure how to tackle it. I am always very vocal at every opportunity I get to articulate the values we have in the school because it won't therefore come as a surprise to anyone when we celebrate Eid or Pride.

Staff colleagues who also have strong views rarely articulate them in the classroom, but it can happen. As a leader you will need to challenge this. As well as an informal conversation, more than once I have followed up with a letter containing a version of this:

> *It has been reported that in a lesson you expressed personal beliefs about conception, abortion, and homosexuality. This greatly upset several students who complained to senior leaders. It is crucial that within any classroom, personal and/or religious beliefs are not shared with students without an alternative perspective being equally shared.*

Colleagues largely understand that sensitive topics can and will be taught and discussed, but balance is essential and discrimination illegal. You have to hold firm but you don't have to go all Darth Vader.

Punk leadership suggests

- That to be a punk leader you have to be committed to inclusivity in the wider sense and you have to be really noisy about it. It should not come as a shock to anyone that you actively welcome children who are refugees, or non-binary, or of traveller heritage, or wear hijabs.
- Your values should be visible, lived by all every day and fully embedded in your curriculum.
- Don't wait for the problem to come to you, know that it already quietly exists and be proactive in fixing it: such as by creating toilets everyone can use.
- Some will call you a woke leader as if it's a slur; embrace it, lean into it and eventually the world will be better for your young people.

16
God Save the Queen
Managing Traditional Expectations

No Future

Is there anyone who doesn't know of The Sex Pistols or of the song 'God Save the Queen'? I was six in the summer of 1977 but I was still very much aware of it, even if my wider family disapproved hugely. It was originally entitled 'No Future' and written by Glen Matlock and John Lydon, although Matlock had been replaced by Sid Vicious by the time the track was released for the Queen's Silver Jubilee. As is punk's evolutionary way, the band's line-up changed quickly as well as the song itself. Guitarist Steve Jones recalls that the first time Matlock played 'God Save the Queen' to him: 'It was like *Love Me Do* or something' (Source: Lonely Boy: Tales from a Sex Pistol by Steve Jones [Wymer Publishing, 2017] Code: 978-0-099510-53-6)

Over the summer I read Steve Jones' autobiography, *Lonely Boy: Tales of a Sex Pistol* (2016). It's not for everyone, particularly if you're not too fond of expletives (lots), sex, drugs and rock 'n' roll. It is, however, a sobering read about the long-term and ongoing impact on someone who was neglected and sexually abused as a child. It is a sober examination of the long-lasting psychological damage inflicted on a child who may not have exhibited as vulnerable, and who is still affected in his sixties.

What was I doing in the summer of 1977? My extended family had moved into a large house together and mum was attempting self-sufficiency as inspired by *The Good Life*. She had goats, chickens, ducks, rabbits and a large vegetable patch. I'd started a new primary school and there we were fully engrossed in all things monarchy during lessons. I got a jubilee souvenir mug. We had some parties. We learnt about divine rule. My nan made a red, white and blue blancmange for a street party and she seemed surprised that no-one really fancied the blue gelatinous food.

I even wrote to the Queen, sending her a picture I'd drawn and when her Lady-in-Waiting responded, my Great Grandad had the letter framed; it's still in the garage somewhere – not because of the Queen, but because of my fondness for Grandad and how excited he was by what now clearly seems a mass-generated letter.

So, it was from this point that I slowly evolved into a Republican even though I grew up nurtured by ardent Monarchists. But people can be like this – forget nature vs. nurture, sometimes beliefs, values and personality traits come from nowhere in particular, although I suppose these views could have been nurtured through a wider exposure to other people in my teen years.

Regardless, the British state education system is just that: run by the state. At the heart of the state is the Monarchy and the Church of England and Parliament, and these *traditional* institutions are at the cornerstone of *Fundamental British Values*.

England's Dreaming

For those of you not working in an English school, the fundamental British values expected to be embedded in every child's educational experience are: *democracy, the rule of law, individual liberty, mutual respect and a tolerance of those of different faiths and beliefs*. Quite rightly, these all sound completely reasonable and very sensible. Indeed, I would take issue with anyone who disagreed that these are good values to teach. My concern is when these values are singularly attached to being British or traditional, or we are gaslit into thinking these are 'traditional British' values that have always been in place when we know that really our history is one of exploitation, plunder and elitism. I mean, why was Dickens successful over a hundred years ago unless he was very adept at pointing this out? You don't stick children up chimneys or down mines unless the *rule of law* says you can. I'm not convinced that a commitment to *democracy* works well alongside a state-funded monarchy and a whole host of other electoral concerns I have. And then, of course, these values are not particularly unique to Britain are they? We are not a floating island of perfect democracy when every other country is a dictatorship.

If you are reading this from another place in the world, or even in time, this may all seem a little odd. It *is* odd.

We are dreaming if we think these are values that have been well embedded in our culture over the centuries (or even the recent decades). Therefore, as school leaders we need to make that dream very tangible: we are instructed to embed these values, make them known to the children, but we also have a commitment to make them relevant to our own communities. The values have to make sense to children's experiences and lives; they have to enrich their futures and make them better citizens of the world.

This is not as easy as putting up some laminated posters and holding an assembly.

Don't Be Told What You Want

These are the fundamental British values we have been dealt and luckily they're not too bad. But how do they fit into our own schools, embracing our own communities? I can't answer that one for you but punk leaders will seize upon this quandary and seek to find a way to make the two things harmonise.

For example, if you work at a faith school, what does *a tolerance of those of different faiths and beliefs* mean to you and your setting? Indeed, what does it mean in a purely secular setting also? Firstly, children need to be taught about a range of different faiths and beliefs, not just their own.

When I was at secondary school 99% of my religious studies lessons were on protestant Christianity with perhaps one lesson on Judaism and one on Catholicism across the three years. This was pre-National Curriculum but it was also very much a school-specific curriculum driven by one evangelical teacher who wanted to save us all from the flames. And I did not attend a faith school. Indeed, most of my education was mono-cultural and pretty much everything has been self-learnt. We owe our children something better. I would hope that attending any school would not prevent actively learning about and appreciating different faiths and cultures and it is a punk leader's duty to ensure that this doesn't happen.

Secondly, *tolerance* is a loaded word to use. According to the OED, to tolerate is to 'To allow to exist or to be done or practised without authoritative interference or molestation; also gen. to allow, permit.'[1] How patronising of the British to adopt a superior position where we allow others to exist, or practice, or believe. It smacks of an elitist Empire where we paternalistically and benignly give permission to those that are not us. Instead, I would argue that an embracing of all people with a range of faiths and beliefs is far more inclusive.

Mutual respect seems like something fairly innocuous; how could anyone disagree with that as a fundamental value? The problem with this one is that you could hesitate for ages waiting for the mutuality. A sort of, *you respect me first* followed by, *No, YOU respect ME first* … Which is bloody useless. Yes, respect that goes both ways is the ideal but it doesn't always work that way, so how about *unconditional positive regard* as advocated by Dave Whitaker in *The Kindness Principle* (2021).

So, you can take something a bit dodgy that you cannot fully subscribe to and make it yours.

All Crimes are Paid

Of course, in recent times *the rule of law* has been very publicly shattered by those who should be seen to uphold it the most. Some of our most high-profile politicians, public servants, celebrities, sports people and even some members of the monarchy have been accused of having no *mutual respect* or adherence to *the rule of law*. It's a very poor example to set for the rest of us. But at least it makes a change from blaming the end of civilised society on single mothers and immigrants.

Without a doubt young people have always been drawn to pushing boundaries and resisting expectations put in place by the Establishment. What you don't want is for them to become criminalised by accident or through design. It has to be far more than dealing with the fallout once a mistake is made, or trying to prevent it through a supercilious approach that only serves to ignite previously dormant rebellious natures.

Proper safeguarding of young people means to fully understand and know your community and the fluctuating issues affecting it; remember these are not set in stone and if antisocial behaviour was the greatest concern regarding your students last year, it could be county lines now and might be substance abuse or domestic violence the following year. Therefore, keep communication channels open with agencies that have a better grasp of this information such as the police, youth services, housing, health, charities and other local schools. And then very sensitively pass this information on to your staff, equipping them with skills to recognise warning signs and what steps to take next. *Keeping Children Safe in Education* (Keeping children safe in education – GOV.UK (www.gov.uk)) has to be contextualised in every setting; it's not an off-the-shelf PowerPoint for the first day's INSET.

Moron

Don't be a moron and think that simply delivering British values verbatim means that is a box ticked. In your own school you will have your own values that are deeply important to you as a leader as well as to your community. Do not sideline them and don't give up on them.

For example, the leaders in our school are completely committed to inclusion. It is possible to combine *a tolerance of those of different faiths and beliefs* (while still challenging 'tolerance') with *respect for those with different identities and backgrounds*: embrace all faiths, beliefs, genders, races, abilities and socio-economic backgrounds.

Punk leadership suggests

....

- It is fine to have a healthy scepticism regarding the institutions we are employed to serve and to remain critical of it regardless of where you personally are on the Monarchy–Republic scale.
- As a starting point, Traditional British Values are eminently sensible for all children so long as you remember that they are not solely British or all that traditional.

- Children and adults should be valued and celebrated at every opportunity. A commitment to one's own faith is to be admired and we all change and shift over time.
- Contextualising the key principles in Traditional British Values is a key safeguarding activity so know your community, make your values relevant and keep them up to date.
- Things change: John Lydon is a Monarchist these days and we're currently singing *God Save the King*.

Note

1   Oxford English Dictionary (2023) *tolerate – quick search results* | Oxford English Dictionary. [online] Available at: https://www.oed.com/search/dictionary/?scope=Entr ies&q=tolerate [Accessed 29 Jan. 2024].

17
I Wanna Be Sedated
Mental Health in Schools

Baby I Love You

In 2003 I got married. Of all the planning, the bit I really enjoyed most was organising the wedding music. The Ramones' cover of 'Baby I Love You' was to be the song we walked back down the aisle to once the vows had been said. Of course, in those days you had to illegally burn a CD in your PC unless you wanted to cart about loads of the original CDs. Preferring the less ethical but far more convenient/cheap approach, I burnt a special 'Wedding Service' CD for the occasion; then promptly left it behind in my PC in Birmingham when the wedding was in Somerset. Thoughtfully, I took the empty CD case so I was completely unaware of the problem until about three minutes before the service started.

To commemorate the rage, there is a wonderful official photograph of me looking like I was about to rip someone's head off and my dad looking terrified, with good cause: he was closest. We had a framed version of it on the wall for years but I'm still furious.

But possibly not as furious as The Ramones were at having to record 'Baby I Love You' in the first place. Originally recorded by The Ronettes in 1963, the story goes that Phil Spector held The Ramones at gunpoint in his house until 4:30am to force the recording. The band refused to play so session musicians laid down the music and Joey reluctantly sang. Unsurprisingly, Joey hated it. Mickey Leigh stated that 'it made me almost embarrassed',[1] and even *Rolling Stone* described as 'a bad idea to begin with, and one that's further burdened by the cheesiest string arrangement this side of the Longines Symphonette'[2] Yeah, its cheesy, but I liked the idea of it for my wedding; it was never to be.

Much more typical of The Ramones is 'I Wanna Be Sedated'. The Ramones are without a doubt one of the cornerstone founders of punk. This is a song written about spending achingly boring days in a London hotel room in the 1970s while the whole city was closed for Christmas. With absolutely everything shut down and only three channels on the telly, we fully understand the sentiment. This chapter is about the punk leadership of mental health in schools; there is a later chapter about punk leaders' own wellbeing.

I Can't Control My Brain

We are beyond crisis point with regard to a mental health crisis not just in schools but in the wider community. It is not just children's wellbeing that leaders have to manage: it is their parents and carers and it is our staff. It's not a secret either; no one has stuck their head in the sand with regard to this particular problem. When *Teacher Tapp* surveyed 10,000 teachers in September 2023 to rank Labour's intended education policies, the top three were related to children's mental health.[3]

There was simply not enough support to go around for all those in crisis or struggling a few years ago, let alone following the trauma of Covid lockdowns. A bubbling emergency has erupted into a full-blown disaster. When children typically spend the vast majority of their time at home, the mental health of those they live with is critical. It is stressful and upsetting to live with others struggling with their own mental health, amplify that if it's your mum or dad. Therefore, children's mental health cannot be managed in isolation as if everyone else in their lives is totally fine, it doesn't work that way. There has to be a proper joined-up approach within the community, but we in schools have little influence over that except to keep shouting about it.

Like everything else, punk leaders have to know what the reality in their own school is. Not what our perception is, because some children present more obviously than others and it is easy to assume that those behaving most extremely are the most affected. This is not always the case, and it is not as transparent as identifying those with the most de-regulated behaviours.

I Can't Control My Fingers

Although I have glibly asserted above that poor mental health does not always present behaviourally, without a doubt it can do. All schools have high expectations that ultimately put some children in conflict with them when they can't (and yes, sometimes won't) comply. The unhelpful and frustrating binary behaviour debate often focuses on whether children are wilfully misbehaving or whether their undesirable behaviours are the consequences of unmet need. Of course, it is both. Some children with poor mental health will misbehave and possibly some of the ways we address these as adults may make these behaviours worse.

Imagine two children in the same class, both of whom are struggling at home. Both are neglected by parents, who have their own problems and self-medicate with alcohol. This weekend their parents were so drunk they forgot to feed their children properly, wash their uniform or check their homework planner or pencil case. Consequently, both arrive at school on Monday without an essential piece of uniform, their planner unsigned and without a pen. When their teacher addresses both, one is quiet and compliant and the other becomes angry, resulting in being asked to leave the room; which is yet more evidence than no one cares. From this point their non-compliance escalates; they are suspended and the cycle continues because their parents are in no fit state to support them either.

Why do those two children react in different ways? I'm not sure any busy school has the skills, expertise or time to fully drill down, although some do and find ways to provide support. Understanding why children behave in a myriad of different ways is key to supporting them and it simply isn't just about clear rules, although firm caring boundaries work for most – it helps them to feel safe.

Nothin' to Do, Nowhere to Go-oh

The services that support young people's mental health are in catastrophic disarray. Poorly funded, they were at breaking point even before the cascade of new cases that are being referred to them post-pandemic. Children and teenagers should not need to be on a waiting list for six months, a year, or even more when they are in crisis. More needs to be done to fund the relevant services, ensuring good quality practitioners are recruited, and stigma is challenged.

Without a doubt, some children are being referred to these services when they don't really recognise their own need, meaning they refuse to engage, creating an impenetrable wall that does more harm than good; and I have seen more than one parent refer their child as a deflection of their own need for parenting support, or to delay referrals to children's services, to then withdraw consent just as the appointment finally comes through. This does little but add to a backlog for the vast majority absolutely screaming out for help.

One solution we use at my current school, and many others are using too, is to employ your own full-time student counsellor. It is not the same as a psychologist or therapist, but it does add tremendous on-site capacity. Being a member of school staff aids the building of relationships, of trust, and it is not seen as unusual to spend some time chatting to a member of the school team. The more members of the school team that are compassionate and care about young people, the safer it is for them. It isn't just one person's role to deal with the difficult children, and all members of staff within a school setting have a role to play. I once saw one of our cleaners lie down on the floor next to a 12-year-old girl in a total meltdown and coax her back to stability. At school, it is everyone's job to support children.

Post-pandemic, being a trauma-informed practitioner is essential. Young people – and their families – and your colleagues – have been traumatised by lockdowns and bereavements.

Before I Go Insane

Supporting young people with poor mental health, as well as wider safeguarding and child protection concerns, certainly has an impact on your own wellbeing. This is why every single school should invest in clinical supervision for their safeguarding team. Largely taken from the field of medicine, where there is open peer review especially when something goes wrong, clinical supervision for safeguarding leads is a process whereby they can speak confidentially about their caseload to someone who has experience in the field. They talk through what has happened, what has been disclosed, what their actions were, how they are feeling about it. Often, the first question of a session will be about anything keeping them awake at night: the child returns to an abusive home, a delay in reporting something, worries that a parent is lying about having food in the house …

Without this service, what else do these frontline workers do to process their experiences and worries? It has an impact on them because they care. Given the confidential nature of what we do, who do you offload to? A colleague? A partner? A friend? Or do you keep it locked up inside you gnawing away?

I'd been a senior leader for ten years, a DSL (designated senior leader for safeguarding) and a headteacher for three years before I even knew that clinical supervision was a thing. Since then, I have ensured that it is provided to all staff that need it. Some choose not to meet with the person we employ for this purpose, more than happy with their own ways to process; others see them every time they are in. And I know some use the time more for personal therapy, but that's alright because it helps them manage a very difficult role in school.

It is even more essential to provide additional support when something catastrophic happens. In my career I have had to lead through the loss of six people, both children and adults; this is many more when adding in parents, children or siblings. All loss is painful but when children take their own lives it is truly wretched. At these times all you can do is keep focused on remaining calm, reassuring the community in an empathetic and sensitive way, whilst taking the time to draw breath. As awful as it sounds, have a plan. I don't know a school that has not experienced loss and having an easily accessible document that identifies who to call and what to do is essential. This is not a time to be freewheeling it. Shut down social media. Do not respond to emotional provocation – some people will say awful things in the heat of the moment or the aftermath of a loss – it is not personal. Do the right thing, even if it is the most exceptionally hard thing.

This is not what anyone in educational leadership signs up for or wants. It's on no leadership course I have ever taken and nothing prepares you for it. I know you will rise to this challenge with love and compassion.

Punk leadership suggests

- Young people's mental health is in crisis – but do you *actually* know what it is like in your own school? Is it a priority?
- Some children will present with extremely challenging behaviours because of poor mental health, and some won't – make sure you understand and support the whole spectrum of behaviour.
- Punk leaders work with as many agencies as it takes to provide effective support for children, families and their own staff – do not attempt this on your own. Help your staff to fit their own oxygen masks through paid-for clinical supervision before they attempt to help children put on theirs.
- Know that at some point a truly awful loss is likely to happen. Have a plan. Keep taking breaths. It'll be OK.

Notes

1   Leigh, M. (2011) *I Slept with Joey Ramone: A Family Memoir*. New York, NY: Simon and Schuster, p. 201.

2   Loder, K. (1980) End of the Century. [online] *Rolling Stone*. Available at: https://www.rollingstone.com/music/music-album-reviews/end-of-the-century-187731   [Accessed 29 Jan. 2024].

3   McInerney, L. (2023) *Labour Party Education Policies: Ranked by Teachers!* [online] Teacher Tapp. Available at: https://teachertapp.co.uk/articles/labour-party-policies-ranked-comparative-judgement/ [Accessed 29 Jan. 2024].

18
She Sells Sanctuary
Finding Your Tribe

The Cult

This is a real belter, especially for an old Goth like me. It's been forty years since I first heard that opening guitar jangle from Billy Duffy and it still sends tingles down my spine. I can play this really loudly every single day and never tire of it; in fact, I probably have. It makes me happy and surely that is an important function of music. The Cult, in pretty much every incarnation they have adopted – from Goth punk *ingénues*, to edgy experimenters, to stadium rockers – have always felt like home; like part of my tribe. They're on every driving-home-from-work playlist I have ever created.

It is important to stress that I use the word *tribe* extremely cautiously. A tribe is certainly a group of people, a community; but historically tribes were united by descent from common ancestors, sharing the same customs and traditions. A tribe is a clutch of aboriginal peoples. Therefore, for me, writing from the land of the oppressor and coloniser, descended from ancestors who destroyed aboriginal tribes across the world, it is distasteful and obscene. And yet I struggle to find a better noun.

I don't mean *colleagues*. After all, many of my professional colleagues have nothing in common with me and enrage me regularly, whether it is their approach to student behaviour and relationships, a disdain for the families I work with or because they are apologists for perverse accountability and stale curriculum.

I also don't mean *friends* or *family*, and frankly many of them have no bloody idea what I do and have little interest even if I start to explain. My friends have other things in common with me which might include music itself, or shared history, or political views. Some of my family I have not spoken to in over ten years and most regard me with increasing disbelief that I haven't ended up in prison or the morgue by now. My dad still does not know what I did at university as he has no frame of reference.

Network is too cold a word for what I mean. It suggests colleagues who are like-minded providing connections to others to build a stronger organisation of professionals. I have some great networks, and some people in my networks become good friends. This chapter is not about networks.

I considered using *cult* too but that is way too loaded with dubious connotations of control and coercion. Without a doubt there are quite a few educational cults, slavish to a charismatic leader and devoted to utter compliance – but I really don't mean that!

So, after a great deal of reflecting and with trepidation I'm going to use *tribe* to describe those people you seek out, or who find you, because you absolutely share the same values and priorities; the same customs and traditions. They feel like family but you have no blood ties. I suppose I mean other punk leaders even if they're more into jazz or hip-hop; even Clannad. I love its warmth, how it confers community and so with heavy heart and multiple apologies I don't culturally appropriate the word *tribe* but rather appreciate it and use as a metaphor.

The World Drags Me Down

Working in schools, especially as a leader, is really hard. It can be draining, demoralising, frustrating and exhausting. Being a leader is simultaneously the best job in the world whilst at the same time you are other people's shit umbrella trying to deflect the bad stuff away from them so they can do their job. Frankly, you can feel dragged down a lot of the time and struggle to get your head above water.

I know that some refer to headship in particular as the loneliest job in a school. Busy, someone always at your door, a million emails and phone calls popping up, always someone in Reception wanting a piece of you, but lonely.

And whilst all of this can be true, it isn't true *all of the time*. Trying to fit into a straight-jacket of what someone else perceives to be the perfect educational leader will only make you more miserable. Punk leaders remain true to themselves, and actively seek out others who are their professional soul mates; their sanctuary and their tribe.

Sanctuary

When I was training as a teacher, I sought camaraderie amongst the other new teaching recruits. Although friendly and usually supportive, it could also be competitive and overhearing people delighting in others' disasters made me uncomfortable. However, thirty years on I am still good friends with fellow trainee Ruth and (Aunty) Liz who was my English Tutor.

Being a newly qualified teacher, I struggled with the rest of the English department who mostly gossiped about their partners, compared diets and bore a grudge against the maths department, so a few of us would go down the pub on a Friday after work for a couple of hours, drink some cider and eat a few packets of Brannigans beef and mustard crisps. I soon learnt that when you fall out with a colleague you can divide a whole staff. Frankly, it's all too exhausting to bother with after a while. I remain extremely suspicious of those that delight in melo-drama in the staffroom.

Initially, social media was a warm and fuzzy place to connect and find like-minded individuals. But you only have to mention something like detentions and the world turns on you. The mute, blog and report buttons have increasingly become my friends despite not wishing to narrow my social networks to a homoge-neous echo chamber and only see posts about biscuits. Although I do like biscuits.

Purple Rage

Research by the Future Leaders Trust in February 2015 that laid bare gender inequality in UK schools was picked up by both educational papers as well as the mainstream media. It caused a bit of a storm on social media, with many of us posting about the issues raised as well as writing blogs. It was not to be the usual storm in a teacup, but persisted, with voices on both sides of the argument truly digging in.

A few of us, fed up of the chatter without action, agreed to meet up to discuss something practical that could be done: and thus, WomenEd was born. We met at a random hotel off the M25 near London for an afternoon tea, pretty much set ourselves up then and there and agreed to organise a small conference. An 'Uncon-ference', said one; we're not macho experts pontificating that we have all the solu-tions, this is a gathering of like minds to explore important and sensitive issues.

On the morning of that first Unconference in London, one of the big male edu-celebrities of the time posted us a *good luck* message, accompanied by an image of women in a bitchy catfight. Ha ha. It was taken down not long afterwards but the resentment and misogyny lingered. Women travelled from all over the UK to attend, most volunteering to speak when they'd never spoken at anything before, not even a department meeting in their own schools; many shook, and kept apologising, or said *I'm not really a proper leader* and the collective support was incredible. Many others came and marvelled that they had never felt so safe, so accepted, and one black woman said she had never been at an educational event when so many people looked like her; usually she was the only woman and the only brown face.

Our first keynote speaker was the wonderful Sue Cowley. In that first delivery she cited her friend's advice to others when they felt scared to take the next step: *Just be ten percent braver*. And that struck such a chord with everyone in the room that we simply adopted it. So powerful was that day, and the ripples it caused on social media, that we knew this could not be a one-off event.

Since then, WomenEd has grown beyond what any of us could have imagined drinking tea and eating egg and cress sandwiches that afternoon. The power of bringing women educators together became an unstoppable machine that saw us grow across the world. To date we have published two books authored by our incredible contributors, we are still holding regional and national (and even global) Unconferences, and we are asked to help shape policy and practice to improve things for women working in schools.

Some of the original co-founders have moved on; after all, we were and are all voluntary and it's a lot of work. No one gets paid. We do this alongside our day jobs and we do it because it is important. At one time or another individuals have had to take a back seat due to the demands in their real lives; at other times, when they have more capacity, they can do more. I liken it to the 1970s Saturday afternoon wrestling on ITV I watched with my nan; get tired, tag out for a bit. Have a rest, tag back in.

Some people have asked me how I have benefited from being involved and whether it has enhanced my career. It has certainly benefited my mental health and wellbeing, it has been a tremendous fountain of support, friendship and allyship. I have learnt so much about women across the world and those in my own school. I was a headteacher on that first afternoon and I am a headteacher writing this now; I do think I am a far better headteacher though and even more committed to creating a truly equitable, inclusive and diverse workforce where everyone feels as if they belong.

One of the most significant things WomenEd aims to tackle is a prevailing sense of imposter syndrome. The irony is not lost on me that I spend most of my time waiting to be found out as a leader, as someone involved in WomenEd, with the other groups I work with. I actually find the Unconferences extremely uncomfortable when people say nice things to me: I think I am a fraud. And it's taken five years to write this bloody book. Punks don't always feel inside how they look on the outside, but we suck it up and keep going because it is important.

The Heads that Turn

When the Headteachers' Roundtable (HTRT) first sent out a call to arms on social media I leapt at the opportunity. A twist of fate meant I could not attend that first meeting (where it looked like it was all men because Ros, the only woman there, took the photo). I thought I'd missed the opportunity but continued to cheer from the sidelines, although I'm not sure I could have behaved myself in a room with Michael Gove.

Through another twist of fate, the then Chair of HTRT Stephen Tierney asked myself and a few others to join the core group and I finally seized the opportunity. I had not met any of them in person beforehand, except Helena Marsh who was a co-founder of WomenEd, and we did feel like the new kids in class. However, meeting them, working alongside them, sharing their troubles and successes has been truly inspirational. Being able to collaborate with the heads of special schools, alternative provision, small nursery schools in affluent areas and other large schools serving deprived communities is educational, illuminating and a privilege.

We get a lot of flak; some think we are not representative of headteachers, and we aren't, intentionally. We are representative only of ourselves; we are not a union or professional body. Again, we're all full-time headteachers (or have been, structures have changed a lot in the last ten years) working in a voluntary capacity to make all of our schools better for every child. That brings a huge sense of achievement.

Punk leadership suggests

- To keep yourself sane and everything in perspective, it is important to find a group of people with whom you can identify and feel safe with.

- You don't need to co-found a horrendously out-of-control grassroots movement, but if you do, know it will consume all your time and you'll still feel like a fraud.

- Remember your tribe is not just for your own benefit; support each other, celebrate each other and give of yourself for the greater good.

19
Pretty in Pink
Looking the Part of Punk Leader

Why Be Pretty?

Technically, I'm not sure whether 'Pretty in Pink' by The Psychedelic Furs is really a punk tune but many of my chosen tracks are similarly dubious. Released originally in 1981, the song became famous following the release of a 1986 Brat Pack film named after it; a more poppy version of the track was re-released and unless you are reasonably old and into post-punk New Wave this is the version you will be most familiar with.

Between 1986 and 1988 I was living in Munich with my parents and sister. My previous only trip abroad was a week camping somewhere in France the summer before. A few days before we were going to leave for this magical holiday my dad 'rolled a Mini to a halt on the hard shoulder of the M4' (police report), severed the tendons in two of his fingers and was in plaster up to his shoulder. This left the driving, on the 'wrong' side of the road, to Mum who had not been abroad herself since she'd been a young teenager in Paris and her fashionable mini-skirt had caused a multi-vehicle pile-up near the Champs Elysees, much to my grandfather's delight.

Regardless, moving abroad was traumatic. I was about to start the Fifth Year (aka Year 11); I was half-way through my O Levels (aka GCSEs) and I had to start again in an international school not really set up for British teenagers. I left behind friends, a culture I was comfortable in and an extended family I'd lived with since I was six. For the first time in a decade I was living only with my immediate family with no escape out to town, or the shops or down a mate's house. We had a TV but before cable and satellite, and without speaking German, there was not much on. We did, however, have video.

My nan would record British TV she thought we'd like and post over to us. We'd watch and post back for re-recording. Once, she sent a mystery film with the note: *Ran out of tape. Man shoots himself.* So not such a mystery anymore.

Probably because she didn't really know what the film was about, and because it had pretty young people on the advertising poster, Nan sent *Pretty in Pink* and it was one of the films we watched a great deal. The film follows the song's sentiment of a woman being used and abandoned by men although the film has a far happier ending with the female protagonist, played by Molly Ringwald, successfully navigating her high school prom.

I never thought that Molly Ringwald *did* look Pretty in Pink; I thought she looked bloody awful but even as a teenager I knew my opinions on what someone else looked like were completely irrelevant and I wasn't going to go down that route, even if I wanted to shout 'NO!' after the line *isn't she pretty in pink?* is refrained. In the film she recycles one of her mother's old dresses into a new gown. Given that at the time I was doing the same but to old curtains and bedsheets, adding artistic shapes with car body paint I found in the garage, that was quite a brave judgement. I looked a bloody state myself.

These days, I do think there is a professional expectation for school staff to dress smartly and appropriately for work. What anyone does in their own time is up to them but while at work I think we have a responsibility to model what suitable work wear looks like, especially if students are in uniform. And as staff model those expectations for young people and their families, so leaders should model for the rest of the staff.

It is not remotely punk at all.

Not So Pretty

What I wear to work is nothing like what I wear in my free time. I like that: two distinct and separate MEs. When I go to work my facial piercings are out, my hair colour is muted, my tattoos are largely covered and, unless it's a million degrees outside, I am in a suit. Trouser suits are my personal preference as tights are evil and I'm a very happy sock wearer.

Without a doubt the best footwear to wear at school is Dr Martens. They are exceptionally hardwearing and comfortable; they are smart; and these days they come in some gorgeous designs. Dr Martens are my last remaining vice. To date I have around 25 pairs and two bags. At one point I did try to vary my footwear but following a particularly wet 90-minute lunch duty while wearing red suede Marks & Spencer pumps, I quit for good. There's nothing like standing up to your ankles in a puddle, more wet than if I'd been barefoot, and staining my lower legs red for days to decide that I'd never wear anything other than Docs again. And regardless of weather or length of duty, I have never been cold or wet since. My mate, Dave Whittaker, a former headteacher in a Pupil Referral Unit, would advise new members of his SLT to invest in a pair of Docs – they were going to need them.

During the longer summer holiday, I choose to dye my hair different colours, usually pink or purple; these can wash out reasonably quickly and get covered by September unlike the persistent blues and greens. This shouldn't be an issue really, I'm pretty much off the clock in August but one painful leadership lesson arose from a pink-haired summer that followed me into autumn.

I used to write a blog, at the time an anonymous safeguarding one. I'd written one about a particularly vulnerable young man, a carer, who had never once had a holiday, not even to visit family in a different town. Someone contacted me to say they wanted to raise some funds to send this young man on a short holiday and, emboldened by *Calendar Girls*, and possibly some gin, they suggested a calendar with teachers posing – not naked and with cakes, but in holiday mode. I was very touched but could not fathom a way to get the money to this young man without identifying him so instead any funds would be donated to a charity that arranged for children with caring responsibilities to go on holiday. They asked if I would like to feature in one of the months.

I agreed and had some photos taken during August: pink hair, tattoos out, facial piercings, pink Dr Martens and reading some poetry. Not thinking, I changed my Facebook profile picture to one of these shots. Although I had my social media locked down, I did not realise that profile pictures on Facebook could still be viewed. Regardless, at the time I didn't really see what the issue was: I was off the clock and this was not an official school account. However, someone shared them widely across the community, determined to shame me for my body size and my appearance and also determined to use them to illustrate the double standards of a student dress code versus staff expectations (because clearly staff codes applied all year round) and made comments along the lines of *look of the fucking state of that* and *fucking fat bitch*.

It gained some traction, as these things do. School shaming in the press is common and teachers are fair game regardless of accuracy or the truth of the matter. For a week it was hell: I had my own crisis manager; I had to phone and threaten to sue a right-wing daily newspaper who used the official photo from the school website and photoshopped it to give me different coloured hair; I received countless death threats on Twitter and via the school website. Worst of all, my face was on the front of the local newspaper and my very young daughter saw it when her dad took her in to get sweets; she became hysterical thinking I was dead.

'This is It, That's the End of the Joke'

Recently, safer recruitment protocols added an online search for any member of staff who applies for a role in a school. We now have a generation of professionals who have grown up with social media and it's likely they have been tagged in pictures and posts from birth upwards. Given this, plus students whose first action once they meet a new teacher is to Google their name, we now have to be ever careful about what these searches will uncover. But to what extent are we as professionals entitled to privacy?

Without a doubt, posting racist comments after a lost football match, sharing misogynistic images online as a joke, contributing to antisemitic Holocaust-denying forums (etc.) is clearly a safeguarding red flag. But twerking at your seventeenth birthday party? Diving into a pool in a bikini? Having pink hair? It's a very thin wedge.

What do you do when you are shamed on social media? I think instinctively the punk in me wants to come out fighting, clawing back some stolen dignity and standing tall. However, you have to play the long game. These people want to provoke you and by responding you often give them exactly what they wanted in the first place. So, starve them of oxygen. Both personal and professional accounts should be locked down, no comment made, don't answer the phone to the press or respond to emails. When the correspondence you receive veers into the downright nasty, offensive or threatening, put it all in a folder and pass it to the police. And yes, you *do* want to press charges because if they're trying to intimidate you they will be doing exactly the same thing to countless others – and you have to take a stand. Be the person who says *no more*.

If you need to respond at all, craft a careful statement and let someone else look over it. Avoid emotive language or hyperbole, remain factual. Once it is shared resolve not to comment further and then you have got to move on, letting the upset and the rage fade away. To ensure this happens, you also have to inform your colleagues of this: when I was informed six months later by a kindly IT technician that *they're hating on you in Thailand now* this was not any use to me at all, it brought it all back.

Then, within your setting, you have to find a way to brush this off – either with a joke, with a hard stare, with planned-ignoring; if it persists you ask someone else to deal with it, such as another senior leader.

> Kid: Is it true you had pink hair?
> Me: I'm far too old for that now. Shall we look at Dickens instead?
> Kid: Can I see your tattoos?
> Me: There are laws about adults showing children bits of their body in school. Now complete your essay.

However, this incident has not stopped me from dressing as I wish in the school holidays or dying my hair. It has not altered my belief that when I am at work I need to dress far more conservatively because I am proudly representing my community and school in a highly professional capacity. But I also don't think that I would have been systemically shamed online had I been male. I am also philosophical that those that went out of their way to troll me would have hated me if I wore a buttoned-down twinset and pearls: haters gonna hate.

As figures of authority (yes, we are), and especially as leaders in schools, you will be targeted by haters at some point in your career; sadly, this is an absolute certainty now. Both for yourself and for those you work with, robust policies and procedures must be in place to respond when something happens. Society has always been cruel. We've loved a public hanging and watching those less fortunate torn apart in amphitheatres from the dawn of time and social media is simply the new incarnation of this. However, the teacher-bashing anecdote down the pub or over the garden wall has now grown to reach an audience of thousands and lasts a lot longer. We owe it to ourselves and our colleagues to simply not stand for it. We cannot pretend we don't see it or hear it, we can't leave others alone to battle hateful comments and we certainly cannot ever think it is justified, even if perhaps someone has been a little bit silly. And there were plenty of those that thought I had been silly and invited such judgement, thus I deserved it.

I am now far more cautious about how to communicate business expectations to my colleagues. I am far clearer to young people and their families about uniform expectations, why we have them and why they might be different for Sixth Formers and staff. I am more hesitant about what I choose to post on social media regardless of how much I lock it down. It doesn't even matter what your expectations are so long as that they are clear and you explain any nuances.

Good strong communication is essential: it is the chorus or refrain in our song, it has to be consistent even if you change the tempo or the key.

Punk leadership suggests:

- Whatever your expectations of staff and students are, make them very clear and over-communicate them.
- It is OK to be fairly traditional and old-fashioned in dress codes if that is important to you and your community.
- Both you and your colleagues will, at some point, be shamed on social media (and/or in the press) so ensure you have an approach to these incidents pre-planned and be strong in your support of others.
- This does not mean you cannot be yourself, there always has to be a gap between the school-you and the home-you, so embrace it.

20
Mommy's Little Monster
Parenting Alongside Leadership

Except, of Course, it Should be *Mummy*

Social Distortion were the trailblazers for Californian surfer-skater punk. Given that I'm not Californian, or a surfer, or a skater, I still really like their rage if not their spelling. Reviewing the album, AllMusic's Paul Tinelli stated that the album shows 'a young punk group that is very angry, and they were going to let society know it whether they wanted to hear it or not'.[1] This is much like having a child.

Although this chapter will explore parenting alongside leadership, I do so from the position of mother not father. Research has shown that there is a fatherhood bonus to leadership earnings, i.e. fathers earn more than non-fathers. However, there is a motherhood-loss, often negatively affecting women who are parents, especially those that take parental leave. The 2015 Future Leaders research showed that 'on reaching headship, mothers are more likely than fathers to start in the bottom third of the advertised pay range, while fathers are far more likely than mothers to start headship in the highest pay band'.[2]

Of course, there are many leaders of all genders who choose not to become parents and many more that are unable. Infertility and baby loss is something I have experienced. I spent a harrowing weekend in Yorkshire on a school trip miscarrying and having to combine attending A&E supported by a confused second in English alongside running poetry workshops and smiling as if nothing was happening. I cried all night but headed into school on Monday morning, convinced my only chance of motherhood had gone, but needing not to be alone with the grief.

By the time I got married we were pretty much certain that we would not be able to have our own children. We went through some fertility treatment, attending a clinic in the same building as the maternity unit, so every visit we had to pass by pregnant mothers standing at the doorway smoking cigarettes. The specialist was coldly dismissive, telling us that there was no point bothering with IVF as the waiting list was too long and we'd be too old by the time we reached the top. I sobbed in the stairwell on our way out and went to work the same day; I did not want to be alone with the grief.

We grew to accept the situation for what it was; we started the process of adoption and the necessary but invasive checking process. We undertook training, we were assigned our own social worker, they started to contact our close friends and family ... and then I fell pregnant.

If it had been anyone else I would have hated me. All through those years of infertility people would tell me stories about women suddenly and unexpectedly falling pregnant after years of trying; these stories, designed to reassure, simply made me feel bitter and resentful – and now it was me. I spent the whole of the pregnancy utterly convinced that I would miscarry. I could not imagine being able to carry a live baby to term, surely something would go wrong. Because of this I did not prepare myself as I should have done. When my daughter was born, I was delighted but emotionally unprepared. Post-natal depression seemed inevitable, I felt overwhelmed by the responsibility and my negative thoughts turned to losing her to cot death or another freak accident. In no way was my becoming a mother a bed of roses and in many ways she was a metaphorical monster whom I loved more than anything but who terrified me beyond belief.

Make Some Noise

I learnt I was pregnant just as I started my first senior leadership role. My headteacher at the time, who had been thoroughly supportive of our adoption journey, was as shocked as anyone, but delighted. Later, as I grappled with returning full-time with post-natal depression, he was just as supportive. My decision to return full-time was one I was always certain of, just as some are certain they won't return at all, or straight away, or full-time. This is a completely personal decision and one that punk leaders should keep the hell out of. I worked up until three days before I was induced and returned after four months. The other women I worked with were incredibly judgemental: *Just four months, are you sure? When the baby is born you'll change your mind. I know someone that had a baby and they were no longer ambitious.*

All of that is fine for other people but it wasn't for me. I'm not virtue signalling; I liked working, being busy, and I knew I would struggle at home all the time by myself with the baby and we would not cope financially. It was no one else's decision and my husband and I were happy with it.

Family-friendly Schools

Schools exist for children and the people that work there care for children every day. So why is it that so often schools are not family friendly for those that work there? Ridiculous start times, end times, out of hours meetings, emails pinging the whole time, no flexibility and a deep suspicion of women of a certain age. It may be illegal, but through WomenEd we have heard about women asked about their birth control plans or family plans during interviews. At the first meeting with a new headteacher I was asked if I was planning more children – it was absolutely not his business. It is not a surprise that the biggest demographic leaving teaching are women in their thirties.

Speaking in 2015, the then chief programme officer at Future Leaders said:

> This has to change. We need more heads who consciously act as role models by being great at their job and shaping it to fit their family commitments, changing school routines to make them compatible with the rhythms of family life. We can't afford for our children to miss out on a pool of exceptional school leaders simply because leadership is seen as incompatible with being a parent.[3]

Schools are not the most flexible of places. After all, if you are a teacher there is a class to teach and they are waiting for you, you cannot be working from home that day. But there are many things punk leaders can do for their staff. Genuinely accepting as many flexible working requests as viable is one such strategy. Too often the barrier cited, especially in primary schools, is that parents don't like their child to have more than one teacher. However, it is far better for a class to have two happy, rested, positive teachers rather than one exhausted and resentful one. Punk leaders tackle parental demands; you can't make the parents love the idea if they don't want to but they'll like losing great teachers to the profession even less. One of the best maths teachers I ever met asked for flexible working after the birth of her first baby; I could have refused but I didn't despite there being a lot of part-time maths teachers already and results needing to improve. But having an amazing maths teacher two days a week was far better than her quitting. She is still with us after three children and we hope one day she will increase her days.

Another common issue we have heard about at WomenEd is that women leaders, upon asking to return to work part-time after maternity leave, are told that they can do this on condition they relinquish their leadership responsibilities, both Teaching and Learning Responsibility payments (TLRs) and those on the leadership scale. This is scandalous and it is blackmail. Punk leaders value all leadership even if it is part-time. I once had a brilliant Assistant Headteacher want to return after maternity leave on three days a week; my boss did not think this was a good idea and some of her colleagues came to me to whisper about the audacity of the woman. But I accepted her request and she had so much impact on the three days she was in. It also freed up some salary to enable a talented middle leader to take on some senior leader responsibilities two days a week; they became a formidable team and the school only benefited.

A woman leader I spoke to recently, who had just returned to work after maternity leave was told by her headteacher line manager that there were two times their line management meeting could take place: 7:00am (before nursery opened) or 5:00pm (nursery would be closed before they got there in traffic). Why would anyone do this? I fully accept the need to meet outside the hours students are on site but this is family-antagonistic and she chose to leave the school rather than compromise her family.

Punk leaders have to do better than this.

How I've Sort of Made it Work (Usually)

Without a doubt, being headteacher made it hugely easier to manage my work and family commitments. On occasion I have been bluntly selfish: my husband had late meetings every Monday so I moved Senior Leadership Team meetings to Tuesdays after school (after checking with the team that this was OK). At the same time, when I asked my team if we could move SLT meetings to a different day, one young father said yes, but that he usually took his sons to football practice that evening. So we did not move the SLT meetings because that time with your children is precious.

I've been very lucky in the sense that my husband is a genuine partner. I remember listening to a female headteacher colleague talk about her decision to divorce. It was when she realised she was essentially raising a man-child as well as her children, and it was draining her, not nourishing her. Supportive structures for your family can come in a million forms and not always through blood or marriage relatives. Bravely, my husband wrote Chapter 9, 'Stand By Your Woman', in *Being 10% Braver* (2021) if you'd like to read his side.[4]

Apart from about six months, since Year 3 my daughter has attended the school I have been headteacher of. I know this will not be for everyone, but it has really worked for us. On both occasions we lived a twenty-minute drive from the school, so close but not in catchment. Certainly, it is a very clear message that I believe in the school I am leading, and am determined to make it good enough for my own child. And I am definitely not playing roulette with her education; these schools, whilst on a journey, have been fantastic for her.

In addition, on two occasions I have also been her teacher. First, I taught her English in Year 9 during the wave after wave of Covid closures and lockdowns. I am currently teaching her A Level Film Studies. You learn a great deal about your child as a student, yourself as a teacher, and the process of learning dialogue through this sort of arrangement. There is *no one* as critical of every element of my lesson plan as my daughter and, once in the car home, she lets rip and frequently does not stop until she's in bed.

To be fair, every aspect of leading a school is open to her searing critique, from the uniform policy, to the times of the school day, to the quality of lunches, to assemblies, to Sports Day arrangements to the choice of musical that year. When she was around ten years old, we had a massive argument in Marks and Spencers (oh the middle-class shame) about uniform as she attempted to convince me that a particular style of skirt was allowed; *but I had written the bloody policy.* No wonder there are so many September local newspaper headlines about uniform compliance disasters.

Not everyone will want their child to attend their school. I was the first to bring mine to this current school and we now have around ten members of staff whose children attend. It can work and it can certainly help.

Punk leadership suggests

· All schools must be family friendly and leaders need to model healthy approaches to work.

· Be aware that frequently there is a motherhood penalty and fatherhood bonus; punk leaders strive to make this equitable.

· It is more than possible to be a parent and a leader at the same time, whether this is full-time or part-time. Part-time leaders are just as brilliant as their full-time counterparts, just not there as often. Take advantage of the opportunities this presents.

Notes

1   www.allmusic.com. (n.d.) *Social Distortion – Mommy's Little Monster Album Reviews, Songs & More | AllMusic.* [online] Available at: https://www.allmusic.com/album/mommys-little-monster-mw0000201296 [Accessed 29 Jan. 2024].

2   SecEd. (2015) *Research Shows 'Motherhood Penalty' for School Leaders.* [online] Available at: https://www.sec-ed.co.uk/content/news/research-shows-motherhood-penalty-for-school-leaders/ [Accessed 29 Jan. 2024].

3   SecEd. (2015) *Research Shows 'Motherhood Penalty' for school leaders.* [online] Available at: https://www.sec-ed.co.uk/content/news/research-shows-motherhood-penalty-for-school-leaders/ [Accessed 29 Jan. 2024].

4   Featherstone, K. and Porritt, V. (eds) (2021) *Being 10% Braver.* London: Sage Publications.

21
Anarchy in the UK
Leading During and After a Pandemic

Right Now

It's a little excessive to have two Sex Pistols tracks as chapter titles, but they are iconic and excess can be great. The mood of this late seventies song is still incredibly relevant, and possibly even more pertinent at the moment.

It is easy to sit back and think: well, the Covid-19 pandemic is over, lockdowns are over, it is no longer applicable to us. But of course, it is. The affected years certainly felt anarchic at the time and, certainly as the government's UK Covid Inquiry progresses, it appears more and more chaotic at the very heart of those institutions making important decisions for the rest of us.

What happened in and to schools during the pandemic is worth exploring, partly to examine and reflect on key decisions we made on the ground at the time; and partly to apply those lessons learnt to future potential disasters (sometimes known as a wet lunchtime in November). There will always be some sort of disaster about to happen. I've also included this chapter because the impact of the pandemic, and the lockdowns in particular, will be long-lasting and more disruptive than we can imagine even now. Last but not least, the whole awful time really revealed how people perceived us in schools – from government ministers to the press to parents. It's a genie not easily shoved back in the bottle.

It's Coming Sometime

The spring of 2020 seems a long time ago now. I'd started as the Headteacher of a school needing urgent turn around just 18 months earlier and we were making good progress. It was a time when, with hindsight, I really loved my job even though it was bloody hard. Before the end of the same year I *hated* it and was on the verge of walking away forever. I was by no means alone in these feelings and the profession, teaching in general and leadership more specifically, has seen many depart feeling burnt out and overwhelmed.

It started as a news story about a virus in China, and I was fairly dismissive when in conversation about it. A student who had returned from a family visit in Poland, who had been given a box of masks at the airport, drove me crazy by handing them out to other students, running in and out of lessons and scaring younger children. When it looked like it was a little more serious, I genuinely believed that schools would be shut down two weeks earlier than the planned Easter break, thus providing a four-week circuit breaker. I was very wrong. But then, no one had experienced anything like it before.

Initially, we arranged for senior leaders and staff volunteers only to supervise our vulnerable learners, children with special educational needs and the children of frontline workers; later we put together a proper rota given how long it was anticipated to last. At the time our biggest conflict with parents was not categorising dog walker or publican as an essential frontline worker. Not many of the eligible children wanted to attend and our greatest fear was whether these most vulnerable of young people were safe. We ensured that every child was telephoned at home at least every two weeks and those we were most worried about far more frequently. We arranged food vouchers, care boxes, and lots of paper-based work to be sent home as not every home had access to a device or the Wi-Fi/data to use it. This was expensive in terms of time and money. An announcement about free laptops caused a flood of demand from parents: we had over six hundred children receiving free school meals; about ten Department for Education laptops arrived – and they did not work.

Managing hybrid learning, fears amongst children, families and staff about their own health and the welfare of those they loved, undertaking personal risk assessments for vulnerable adults, arranging alternative provision when staff were shielding, trying to source and provide appropriate PPE, undertaking wave after wave of track and trace, ensuring everyone was getting enough to eat, managing the sudden unemployment of huge numbers of parents/carers and trying to get my head around ever-changing guidance. I cannot tell you how many times I updated our school-specific Covid Risk Assessment; looking through my folders there are at least fifty-plus versions and I always wondered whether anyone actually read them.

No Dogsbody

At the start, there was a lot of social media chatter from parents laughing that teaching was *actually* hard work and that they were glad they didn't have to do it very often; weren't teachers great? At some point this changed. Schools are very accessible places. When you can't contact the doctor, or housing, the police, or the bank, or your job, you can definitely contact school. We bore the brunt of a lot of rage. Understandably, everyone was anxious; parents wanted their children back at school, they wanted to go out and work, and it was very easy to revert to a lazy-teachers stereotype, especially if someone tested positive and the whole bubble had to go home to self-isolate. Even the police phoned us to complain: could we please ask our students to stay home and self-isolate rather than congregate down the park? Yes, we had asked them.

Compound this with the divisive nature of wearing masks, regular testing, social distancing and closing down bubbles and the scene was set for schools to be in almost continual conflict with parents and the wider community. The guidance told us that all those except the most vulnerable to anxiety or breathing problems should be wearing masks in closed spaces, such as corridors and, given how many clinically vulnerable people we had at school, we insisted on this very firmly. Queue huge numbers of children and their families who went to war with us over this. Previously delightful families were on social media whipping up hate campaigns against the school regarding the infringements of their child's rights *not* to wear masks if they didn't want to. Some schools simply did not enforce it, they did not want the rage, and who can blame them?

Then throw into the mix that the then Secretary of State for Education suggested to parents that if they were unhappy with *anything* their child's school did, they should complain directly to Ofsted. Oh my word did the heavens open. A never-ending thanks for that, Gavin.

Anarchy

Through the autumn of 2020 and the winter of 2021, the guidance changed far too regularly to keep up to date with. The Department of Education seemed hell-bent on outdoing themselves with how many times they could change their minds and how antisocial they could be with the timing of their guidance. Open. Shut. Bubbles. Masks. Tests. Teacher Assessed Grades. Centre Assessed Grades. Contextual adjustments. OK, no change. Last minute on a Friday afternoon. Just as the Christmas holidays began. Or ended. Threats of legal action if schools chose to shut followed by an immediate decision that schools now had to shut whether they wanted to or not. It felt like anarchy; as video footage and WhatsApp messages from within the heart of government emerge, we know that it genuinely was anarchy. Utterly clueless and extremely dangerous.

Worse still was when the WhatsApp messages between Gavin Williamson and Matt Hancock were released;[1] many had long suspected the profession was held in contempt by ministers, but seeing the contempt laid bare was extremely hurtful.

Of course, those making these decisions were not actually in schools having to implement their decisions. That was us, the leaders, and none of us actually wanted anarchy, not even the punks.

What did we do at this time that we can now reflect and learn from?

We worked as a team – both within our schools, across local authorities, trusts, on social media and through professional associations; the NAHT and ASCL worked overtime for us and it felt like they were alone in fighting for us. We learnt from each other and took good ideas and applied them to our own contexts. It didn't matter which school was primary or secondary, maintained or an academy, mainstream or special – we collaborated.

We recognised when each of us was approaching burn out and supported without question. I needed to be at school and to be busy, others left me to get on with it even on the days being busy meant I interfered.

We really appreciated the importance of family: some of us lost some of our own family members, we saw children lose relatives, relationships crumbled and jobs were lost. We had to be compassionate at a time when we were all fatigued. The headteacher of a local school, who had held on well after the usual retirement age, and who was finally about to hang up his chalk, contracted Covid and died in hospital. A student whose only carer was his nan lost her to Covid and still, over two years later, there is no one with official parental responsibility for him. Some students remained locked in abusive homes and the danger only got worse.

We are still putting things back together and will be for a long time, but we must continue to reflect on how we adapted and pulled together at this time to remember we can achieve pretty much anything.

Destroy

The impact of this time on both young people and the adults in their lives has been at best horrible and at worst catastrophic. Lost learning is the very least of it and there is no way to simply catch up; if catching up on two years of disrupted learning was easy, every school would be streamlining their approach to achieve these ends anyway. Young heads are not empty vessels to be filled with knowledge; even less so can their empty heads simply be paused like a recording, easily turned on and off.

The disruption to young people's lives, learning, families, mental and physical health has been cataclysmic. We cannot judge their recovery from the pandemic through end of key stage assessments, nor through Phonics Testing, SATs, GCSEs or A Levels. Oooo look, GCSE pass-rates at back to 2019 levels, it's all over.

We have children starting nursery now that were born during the pandemic and who have rarely left the house. They have not been seeing health visitors, who are back-logged anyway, and are now starting school with little experience of interacting with other children or adults and with less developed language skills;

some are not toilet trained and some have misshapen mouths as they've had their dummy in for far too long.

We have children of all ages who don't really want to leave the safety of their bedrooms and believe education is accessing a few apps or reading some online material. The online material that many of them have been accessing is far from ideal and so we have seen explosions of sexual coercion, online hatred and the polarisations of opinions. Some parents no longer prioritise good attendance at school – after all, what is the point because they did fine during lockdowns and *they* are working from home fine too? We have many children and adults who are less able to self-regulate, which, when you're in a school of hundreds, does not make it the friendliest or safest place to be.

There are no easy solutions to any of this, despite popular beliefs to the contrary. In ten, fifteen years the impact of Covid will still be affecting the population regardless of exam results. However, one thing we must do in schools is not simply reset our expectations to how things were prior to spring 2020; this is now a completely new state of being and the old world has been destroyed. We therefore have a chance to build back better: more measured, more compassionate, more inclusive, more creative, better resourced. We punk leaders have our time to shine.

Punk leadership suggests

- It is worth spending some time reflecting on what you, your school and your colleagues went through during the pandemic even if it is upsetting, to examine just how incredible we were and how many achievements were successful.
- Take these reflections and consider how we can use them to model best leadership practice going forward.
- What is your new world *really* like?
- How can we all lead our schools to become better in this new context?

Note

1   Weale, S. (2023) Teachers Say Gavin Williamson Pandemic Texts Reveal 'Secret Contempt'. *The Guardian*. [online] 2 Mar. Available at: https://www.theguardian.com/education/2023/mar/02/teachers-gavin-williamson-pandemic-matt-hancock-texts-secret-contempt [Accessed 29 Jan. 2024].

22
Living Dead
Managing Your Own Wellbeing as a Leader

Plasmatics

Coming out of the late seventies New York punk scene, the Plasmatics were extremely chaotic, theatrical, anarchic and sexual. Writing in *Louder*, Chris Knowles describes the band as 'middle America's worst nightmare, in living, lurid colour: Sodom and Gomorrah on the march'.[1] Despite the whole band emerging from manager Rod Swenson's theatre show *Captain Kink's Sex Fantasy Theatre*, it was lead singer Wendy O. Williams that was the target of sexist critics, with one writing that, 'lead singer/ex-porn star/current weightlifter Wendy Orleans Williams (W.O.W. for short) spends most of the Plasmatics' show fondling her family-size breasts, scratching her sweaty snatch and eating the drum kit, among other playful events'.[2]

In 1991 Wendy gave up the punk limelight, moving to Connecticut to work as an animal rehabilitator, explaining that she 'was pretty fed up dealing with people'.[3] She died by suicide in 1998, at her third attempt in four years. Swenson, her partner of more than twenty years, explained that, 'Wendy's act was not an irrational in-the-moment act'.[4]

Whilst other punks were angry or anti-establishment or challenging gender roles, the Plasmatics were being arrested, beaten up and exploding cars on stage. As punk leaders go, they genuinely were living their values, not just laminating them.

I Tried to Warn You

As we have established, school leadership can feel a little like a Plasmatics live show. Things *happen* every day and very rarely are they what you plan to happen. For example, a lunchtime supervisor has just dropped off at my office a clock he found Sellotaped to a tree; this is not what one would normally expect and I now need to reunite the clock with its classroom.

Schools are brilliant places to work. No two days are ever alike, not just across the week but across an entire career. Kids are *brilliant*: eager, funny, keen, clever, dynamic, creative, surprising … as well as occasionally frustrating or hurtful. The adults that work alongside you are dedicated, hard-working, ambitious and inspirational … and sometimes awkward or stubborn. The majority of your time working in a school will be fantastic if exhausting. You will need those holidays because otherwise you would literally collapse and never get back up. The relationships you build within the community are mostly warm and reciprocal; sometimes, like family, people will drive you nuts. You will, over time, feel as if you are making a difference and people's lives are better for you having worked with them.

But there is another side, and no one would pretend otherwise. If it was all peachy there would not be a recruitment and retention crisis at the moment. As explored through the whole of this book, schools can also be challenging places to work. As wonderful as they are, children, their families and your colleagues can also drain you, exhaust you and upset you.

The pressures put upon school leaders are unsustainable: curriculum changes, meeting the needs of all children, post-Covid behaviour, constant criticism, social media, litigation, funding, recruitment, retention, outcomes, attendance, Ofsted, local authorities, multi-academy trusts, pressure groups, the DfE … If all these things exist for everyone working in a school, they weigh particularly heavy on the shoulders of leaders.

I Could Not Stop You

School leaders tend to have been promoted to these positions from non-leadership roles. Frankly, school leaders *should* know what they're getting into. But knowing what is waiting for you, and dealing with it are two different things. It's like being a parent to a new-born and being helpfully reminded through the colic, w*ell, I did warn you it'd be like this …*

We must be honest with ourselves about the stresses and pressures of being a school leader. As a punk leader you will acknowledge this for yourself and for those you work with. We are human and occasionally those stresses and pressures can tip into something darker and more pervasive.

It is not just work that can affect your mental health but we spend so many hours working, on things that really matter, for children that deserve only the best, it will always be a huge factor. The anxiety caused by sitting in the Ofsted inspection window is so great that many heads turn to medication. The despair caused by poor results, or an inadequate inspection can lead to worse. Again, knowing these things are possible, and dealing with them, are two different things.

Many organisations have sprung up to support school leaders, especially head-teachers over the past few years, all amazing. Groups like Headrest and Heads Up for Headteachers are a literal lifeline to colleagues. Professional associations such as NAHT and ASCL have their own offer, as well as provision from local authorities and trusts. Everyone working in this sector is inundated with need and the stories that leak out are heart breaking. The attrition in the workforce is not survivable. We know some colleagues have quit, retired early, turned to alcohol and substance abuse, damaged personal relationships and some have hurt them-selves. Largely, these are pressures that can be alleviated by those in positions of power through a system-wide and revolutionary change to our experience. We need to blow the car up on stage.

In Your Head

Being honest about your own mental health requires a great deal of bravery. Tell-ing someone about it is heroic.

Your own mental health is a very private matter and when you are unwell you may not wish to even acknowledge it yourself. When I was interviewed by Iesha Small for her amazing book *The Unexpected Leader* (2019) I was not expecting to be so candid about my own struggles with post-natal depression and the impact it had on my personal and professional life. Naively, it also did not dawn on me that perhaps other people would read about it – even my mum. So I wasn't being particularly brave, but Iesha is super intelligent, wonderfully warm and disarm-ing. And, with hindsight, I might have been a bit bloody stupid.

Without a doubt, my own mental health has never been great and it wasn't long before the post-natal depression got me. I have experienced teenage-trauma, university-blues, single-woman-miseries, getting-older-sadness, menopause-madness, bereavements, financial-worries, relationship-woes, some professional post-traumatic disorder terrors and the lying in bed at night wondering if it all wouldn't be bet-ter if the world stopped spinning and we all fell off. I have experienced depres-sion, anxiety, a terrible sense of doom and suicidal thoughts. I have experienced medication, talking therapies, people telling me to get my shit together as well as holding me while I sobbed. Nothing has ever really been *diagnosed*.

All through this I just kept going. I don't think I have ever taken a single day off work because of poor mental health. For me, working is a wonderful distraction and it occupies a mind that has always been prone to darkness. Maybe it's why I was a Goth.

Certainly, I am not alone. *We* are not alone.

Having poor mental health should not preclude anyone from a career in school leadership unless you take your mood out on children, their families or your colleagues. We have all seen that and some of us have experienced it. I once worked at a school where a maths teacher would abandon her classes at the end of my corridor, come into my office and start bawling. A friend worked with a headteacher who would scream at his senior team when under pressure and the following week buy them cakes and make jokes. Many years ago I knew of a Head of Department who grabbed a child by the throat and pinned him against the wall, Darth Vader-style, because he was bottling up that his wife had left him.

Many people in all sorts of jobs, but definitely teachers, suffer from Sunday night blues; that sinking despair as the weekend runs out, sleep is disrupted and the morning alarm comes too soon. Increasingly, I know of people who experience the Friday afternoon fear; knowing they will be going home either alone, or to a lonely house, without much money and nothing really to do until Monday.

Society has become very insular: too much shielding, isolating, staying at home, and catching up on Zoom. At the first large social event post-lockdown, a conference in Birmingham, I ran around like a puppy with the zoomies, drinking too quickly, talking to people I hadn't seen in a couple of years and then pretty much collapsing. During a second event in London I experienced a huge panic attack and hyperventilated in a toilet before managing to get outside. However, this has never happened at school, even during horrendous interactions or dealing with traumatic issues.

Living Dead

Don't live dead, enjoy what you do. If not right this second, in the future sometime. Don't let others live dead either, certainly not because of the conditions you create at your school or for your team. Punk leaders are better than that. When the job brings you no joy, leave. You deserve better and the children deserve better.

Check in with your staff regularly and don't get fobbed off by glib responses and fake smiles. Find myriad ways to bring people together: a book club, a homemade curry after work, a quick beer down the pub, walking the corridors with a tub of sweeties for those needing a sugar-hit, playing a happy tune at the start of meetings and also letting people opt out of the jollity. There are few things more miserable than one of those enforced wellbeing days where you are made to do yoga. Never force anyone to do anything that will make them *more* miserable. Except for marking. We all need to do marking.

> ## Punk leadership suggests
>
> ....
>
> - You have to walk into every role with your eyes wide open, appreciating both the beauty and the horror of what it might entail.
> - Be honest, at least with yourself, about your own mental health and what to do if and when you struggle.
> - Call upon those with the power to change our conditions to do so, and don't let up until they do.
> - Know that you are not alone and by supporting each other we can get stronger. Other leaders, other headteachers and definitely other people in your setting will be struggling every day. Acknowledge that and do what you can to catch each other before you fall.

Sources of Support

- Headrest: headrestuk.co.uk
- Heads Up For Headteachers: headsup4hts.co.uk
- Mentally Healthy Schools: mentallyhealthyschools.org.uk
- Education Support: educationsupport.org.uk
- Mind: mind.org.uk
- Samaritans: samaritans.org

Notes

1 Knowles, C. (2023) *The Story of Wendy O Williams and the Plasmatics: 'I Woke up in a Pool of Blood on the Way to the hosPital'*. [online] Louder. Available at: https://www.loudersound.com/features/wendy-o-williams-the-plasmatics-story. [Accessed 29 Jan. 2024].

2 Gimarc, G. (2005) *Punk Diary: The Ultimate Trainspotter's Guide to Underground Rock 1970–1982*. Essex, CT: Backbeat Books.

3 Keedle, J. (1998) *'Wendy O., We Hardly Knew You'*. Hartford Advocate. December 5. Available at: http://www.hartfordadvocate.com/articles/wendyo.html [Accessed 29 Jan. 2024].

4 The Columbian (1998) Former Punk-Band Singer Wendy O. Williams Dies. *The Columbian*. April 9.

23
Happy Talk
Keeping Sane and Maintaining Your Principles

He Said Captain, I Said 'Wot?'

Punk legend Captain Sensible had an unlikely solo UK number one in 1982 with the South Pacific song 'Happy Talk' and did so without resorting to a similar bastardisation as Sid Vicious employed with 'My Way'. I remember watching him on Top of the Pops with my nan who laughed, 'He is silly but I do like him.'

Captain Sensible, so named because he was anything but sensible, joined The Damned in 1976, the first punk band to actually release vinyl, although he temporarily left in the eighties. Like all punk leaders he did what was necessary and played bass, keyboards, lead guitar and quickly became the primary songwriter. He's an accomplished musician regardless of any assumed chaos and even now as he approaches 70 he is still doing what he loves and is seemingly as comfortable with beer-on-the-head punk as he is with Rodgers and Hammerstein. He's a man who, when despairing of UK politics started his own political party, putting his money where his mouth was and remaining completely committed to democracy.

Speaking in 2012, the Captain said, 'Punk should be more than the music, it's an attitude which says regardless of your circumstances you can be creative and make something of your life.'[1]

Likewise, punk leadership is not only about education, it's about creating the conditions for yourself, and all those around you to be creative and to make something of their lives, especially the kids. Not for the first time, punk has been defined as not merely a subculture but an all pervasive and long-lasting attitude with which to approach life. It's low-tech, it's raw and authentic and it's about getting stuff done yourself, even if it's well out of your comfort zone.

In the same way as we should not teach to the test we should not lead to the inspection.

What can we learn from the Captain about being a punk leader?

Punk leaders get good at it: early punks were not great at their craft but they stuck with it, they kept practising and got really good. They knew their ideas were important enough to improve the vehicle to deliver their messages. And punk leaders always have a purpose.

Punk Leaders are part of a team: Not many solo punks; Patti Smith perhaps? Captain went solo but he came back to The Damned, and thank God he did.

Punk leaders are flexible: Captain started off as the bassist and when needed moved to guitar. Sometimes he also sang. There have been many many line-ups of The Damned and being a flexible leader means you work with different people in different shapes to get the job done. Often, something will go wrong on stage, such as a string snapping or going out of tune; no need to throw a diva tantrum, it's all part of the craft and so long as you work to fix it most things are resolvable.

Punk leadership is not positional: in most bands the lead singer acts as the leader; Dave Vanian is a brilliant front man but on stage you get the sense that Captain is directing: the first on, the most vocal between tracks, lots of banter with the crowd and then the last off. Leadership is more than a position; you're part of a band and you're there for the audience.

Punk leaders love what they do: it's meant to be fun. Not every day will be brilliant but overall it's got to be worth sticking with. Over 45 years later Captain is still writing, recording and touring with as much gusto as in 1976. Never take it too seriously even if what you're doing is important.

But, Punk leaders smash it up: we stick our necks out, we take risks, when the system is not working for children we work relentlessly to improve it even if that's a bit of a hassle. We 'scream and shout til [our] dying breath'.

Have a Dream

In schools when we articulate vision it tends to be very specific to our own school context, and that's fine. But too often vision statements can sound vague, glib and their only purpose is to be laminated for display rather than for living. That's absurd. We are more likely to teach Martin Luther King's *I Have a Dream* as technical rhetoric than as a brilliant model for articulating our own personal dreams. And unless you have a dream how will it ever come true?

So, what is your dream – your real dream – for education? What would you say at interview if you were guaranteed to get the job, or if money was no object, or if league tables were not published? In the same way no child has ever run in excitedly from break to copy down a learning objective, surely no one has ever jumped out of bed and rushed to work to improve their Progress-8 score by 0.1, especially given that would shunt another school down by −0.1?

At my most generous I also hope no one's dream is to alienate children by not including them but I also know of too many schools that deter children with special needs from applying and smile as they tell parents that 'X school down the road is far better at meeting their needs'. I'd hope all leaders would want to celebrate and develop all professionals in school but I also know colleagues who have been bullied and sidelined until they've left. Many have completely left the profession, there's even a few Facebook groups celebrating new starts. It's not like we have loads of teachers floating about. Surely no one's dream is to quash others?

Happy Talk

Teachers are often their own worst enemies, resigned to awful self-fulfilling prophecies. Yes, the job is hard but it is also extremely rewarding. There are ridiculous lows but unimaginable highs. The role you play in the lives of young people is an utter privilege; you will change those lives and make a difference forever. But as a profession we don't spend enough time talking about the sheer delight of the job and instead let the negative press and constant social media hatred press us down; particularly if we shut due to weather, are striking for better pay and conditions or are affected by a global pandemic. Understandable as this is, we have to reflect on what should carry more weight – our own professional pride and the positive impact of this professionalism on children's lives *or* the vacuous negativity of strangers who could never do the job themselves?

We simply have to talk more positively about our careers and what is awesome about our job. It means when young people say they want to become teachers we don't wrinkle our noses and do our best to talk them out of it. It means when one of your friends slags off teachers (and the holidays) you step up and challenge it. It means if you see a stupid and thoughtless comment on social media you gently call it out and explain why they're wrong. It means when our colleagues sit in the staffroom and slag off others you tackle it or do something actively to improve matters.

It also means that sometimes you have to take a deep breath and seek promotion to leadership, including headship.

Happy Doing

Happy talking is essential but probably more important to your everyday wellbeing is to be happy doing things. Talking, thinking, strategising, envisioning is all great but unless you get on and *do things* then leadership becomes a concept not a role. Leaders have to lead people who are also doing things, similar things, otherwise leadership is just thinking out loud in an echo chamber where nothing ever escapes, just great thoughts bouncing around an empty room.

Teachers, like many other professions, like to be led by people that have demonstrated that they have previously *done the thing* that they are currently employed to do, and ideally have done it well. That's why there is so much hostility towards non-teachers who have aspirations towards headship or becoming a CEO of a Trust. How can a former HR manager understand the time pressures of lesson planning and marking? How can an accountant comprehend the emotional impact of a safeguarding disclosure? How can a business entrepreneur fully appreciate the complicated context that influences student outcomes? It is not as if being an architect or dentist prepares you for gate duty. Although there are some professions that are more compatible than others, such as public services, the journey through a school is a perceived essential rite of passage for leadership.

So, pretty much like all those future musicians who at the dawn of punk picked up an instrument with no knowledge or skill whatsoever and just decided to make music anyway, so it is for punk leaders. You are never fully prepared for your new role no matter what level it is. However, an absolute determination to practise until you're good is crucial. Your colleagues will be sympathetic towards you as you start, but you have to take it seriously, you have to graft to improve and you have to be open to learning from others regardless of their supposed place in the hierarchy.

What you do to make you happy both in and outside of work is always important. We have to retain ultimate responsibility for our own happiness; we retain agency over key decisions after all and the boon of being in the middle of a recruitment and retention crisis is that if you are being poorly treated where you are right now someone else is desperate for you and will treat you much better. Do not feel stuck where you are. More than once I have resigned with nothing to go to and something suitable has come along at the right time.

For teachers, teaching should make you happy. It's not always a shared value across the industry but at my school all leaders teach, especially me. As a headteacher I have always taught and I believe all heads should teach. As I write this, I am temporarily an Executive Headteacher, undertaking a community project, and for the first time in around thirty years I am not teaching. Bloody hell I miss it. And I will definitely be picking up teaching again when the role is done. Doing cover is not the same; duties are not the same; staffing detentions or the behaviour recovery room is not the same.

Punk leaders still get their hands dirty with the business of planning, teaching, marking, data entry, classroom management, rewards, slippery seating plans, calls home to parents, parents' evenings and, most importantly, being able to take the temperature in our classrooms on a regular basis: what's working well, where are the stressors, how can we make things better for all stakeholders, how are things on the corridor? Continuing to teach is important for our own wellbeing, for the benefit of the school as leaders tend to be more experienced in the classroom, and for the rest of the workforce – they all know that I am experiencing what they are even if it's on a more occasional basis. If we introduce a new approach to teaching and learning then it also applies to me; from my position in the classroom I have to be convinced it will make things better.

Big Mouth

There is an added responsibility for some with a more prominent platform to speak a little more loudly sometimes.

As leaders we have the added responsibility to make the dream come true for as many people as possible. I'm not stupid enough to imagine we should take responsibility for making *everyone* happy; frankly, I can't even do this for myself consistently. But we can talk up the job, the kids, emphasise the benefits and be relentlessly positive. When Vic Goddard speaks to other headteachers, he says, 'Remember we make the weather.' We must choose to be the sun, not the rain and never the storm even when we're feeling drizzly.

We have a responsibility to our own communities of course, but our communities extend far beyond the school gates, or town limits and even national borders. No one should celebrate another's school getting poor results or a damaging Ofsted report. We as educators should never lift ourselves by rejoicing in others' difficulties or even contributing to them. The same weekend that the heart-breaking news of a headteacher suicide following an inadequate inspection by Ofsted hit the news, I saw leaders still posting screenshots on social media of their own fantastic Ofsted reports. Although I appreciate the desire to celebrate success, especially if it follows a period under special measures or being judged as inadequate, the awfulness of the impact of those lesser judgements, particularly for schools being downgraded, is shocking. These are real people, with families and friends, who now feel that *they* as a person are inadequate and have shamed their school community. This has to stop. And we have to find a way to celebrate success without making failure worse to endure.

Will being a punk leader make you happy? Not necessarily, but it should make you *happier*. There's not much that can make you happy if you're doing a two-hour lunch duty in the rain, or breaking up a fight, or dealing with angry parents in Reception, or conducting a home visit to find the furniture and carpets have been repossessed, or as you lie awake the night before you download results, or when tragedy takes one of your community. But if you are leading as yourself and not some grey cookie-cutter replica who jettisons their values for a percentage point, if you can always put your hand on your heart and know what you're doing is the best possible thing for your children and that you've given it everything you've got even if you're not entirely sure if it's going to work out, then you're a punk leader.

This is how we have a dream come true.

Punk leadership suggests

....

- That punk leaders consciously craft a happy school environment for themselves, for their colleagues and also the children.
- Be very clear about how you articulate your dream, your vision for your school or the area in which you lead. If it is clear, and repeated, it can be shared; a refrain is essential.
- Talk about your role, your school and the profession positively; stress your pride at being part of an amazing team and let's change some of the popular narratives about lazy teachers with lots of holidays – we change lives!
- Keep teaching as it should make you happy, and keep being great at it.

Note

1   Hendicott, J. (2012) *Interview: Captain Sensible (The Damned) – James Hendicott.* [online] Available at: https://www.hendicottwriting.com/music/interview-captain-sensible-the-damned/ [Accessed 29 Jan. 2024].

Afterword – Take Me I'm Yours[1]

Hywel Roberts

[Punk rock is] lunging after some glimpse of a new and better world.
(Lester Bangs)[2]

I was cognisant of the existence of the punk movement when shopping with my Dad, in Presto's supermarket in Manchester in the latter part of the 1970s. There was a guy who worked stacking shelves. He had a most impressive hairstyle, shaved at the sides, then lifted to a spike down the centre. As we would approach him up the aisle with our wobbly trolley, my Dad would whisper to us, 'Here's Martin'.

Martin was the first punk I had ever met. He looked scary but always let his face break into a grin when he saw us. I still would move behind the protective shield of my Dad's legs to hide from his gaze. I wouldn't listen to what they talked about, Martin and my Dad, and I didn't really know how my old man would know such a person. I was too focused staring at Martin's huge boots. It must've taken him all day to get them on! Turns out, Martin the Punk liked my Dad.

When they finished their little exchange, we would continue up the aisle and my Dad would say, 'Good old Martin' to nobody in particular.

My Dad was Martin's form teacher when he was at school. This happened every time we went shopping for a good while. This lovely exchange. This seeming clash of culture.

When home in Manchester these days, and as I stare into the abyss of my mid-fifties, I do wonder what became of those punks of old.[3] Like Martin. Those kids on the streets, with their make-up and their hair frozen in time for future photography exhibitions and Julien Temple documentary retrospectives. They're all much older now but are still hanging on to the philosophies and beliefs that made much of the movement so good for social change, development and action.

And now this book is in your hand, I wonder what you will do with it.

We're all looking askance at you, with our lips slightly curled, waiting.

Keziah has played her part and played it well. Rather than smash the system, she's offered you a way to work within it, to navigate it. Education is complex and we all need maps to help us find our way. One of the reasons The Sex Pistols imploded was they had no direction, which could be seen as punk, but it was a chaotic spiral downwards. School ecosystems need more than slogans in order to have a chance of running smoothly; they need more than published curricula or A4 laminated behaviour policies; they need people. A school, like a community, like a movement, a belief system, needs people to help it thrive. Keziah has prompted your thinking about such things in *Punk Leadership* and now it's over to you.

Some things to consider:

- What's the soundtrack to your leadership?
- The roots of punk go back to the 1960s. When does your leadership journey begin and how do you want it to develop?
- What do you hold dear in your work in school?
- What do you bring to your work in school?
- What do you want your legacy to be to the school?
- What can you do to keep to your own values and beliefs about education?
- How does the curriculum in your school reflect these values and beliefs?

And finally…

- What do you want it to be like to be led by you?

Punk could be seen as unwieldly, frightening and combative in its day. *Punk Leadership* is an act of love.

Hywel Roberts is a teacher and writer. His latest book, 'Botheredness', is published by Crown House. He plays bass guitar and runs a brewery. Find him at http://botheredness.co.uk

Notes

1   Squeeze (1978) A bridge song taking us from punk to new wave.
2   Bangs, L. (1977) Lester Bangs Falls in Love (and Sees the Promised Land), *New Musical Express*, 10 December, pp. 31–4.
3   See also the punks on the London Underground in John Landis' *An American Werewolf in London* (1980).

INDEX